DISCARDED

SAVANNAH

By Betsy Fancher

SAVANNAH
THE LOST LEGACY OF GEORGIA'S GOLDEN ISLES
BLUE RIVER

For Jim,
with love

ACKNOWLEDGMENTS

The author is deeply indebted to those who helped along the way, most especially to Ewald Kockritz, a Miamian who long ago fell in love with Savannah and acted as my guide in exploring the town. Then there were Mary Knapp of the Atlanta Public Library and the fine staff of the Savannah Library and so many others: Judge Alex Lawrence, whose research for his book *A Present for Mr. Lincoln* proved invaluable to me; Lee Griffin, the writer; Betty Platt, formerly of the Savannah Chamber of Commerce; Betty Rauers, who co-authored the little guide book *Sojourn in Savannah*; Mrs. Lawrence Lee, of Historic Savannah; Herb Traub, of "the Pirates' House"; Miss Anna Hunter, who pioneered Historic Savannah; banker Mills B. Lane, whose benevolence has helped transform the face of the city; my aunt, author, appraiser and lecturer, Will H. Theus; historian Jim Whitnel, whose private library of out-of-print books was a rare and important source for me.

Also, there were Lee Adler, the veritable backbone of Historic Savannah; Laurie Abbot and John McGowan, pioneers of Skidaway; Mrs. Lilla M. Hawes, who heads the Georgia Historical Society; Jim Williams, the entrepreneur who has also made his distinguished mark on the city; Lionel and Julie Drew and their daughter Becky, who contributed the research on Savannah ghosts; Ross Ingram; Miss Bessie Lewis, noted historian; Dixon Preston, who typed and sometimes edited the manuscript; Mayor John Rousakis, who quite gallantly presented me with the key to the city; my friend and physician, Frank Pittman, and my husband, Jim Fancher, for their unflagging encouragement.

CONTENTS

1	Savannah: An Introduction	1
2	Founding	5
3	The Revolution	13
4	The Code Duello	23
5	Of Slavery and the Wanderer	43
6	Fort Pulaski	57
7	THE War	65
8	Savannah Ghosts	79
9	Savannah's Architecture	91
10	Pollution and the Water Lords	101
11	Resorts	109
12	Savannah and Conrad Aiken	117
13	Skidaway Island	127
14	Dining and Drinking in Savannah	133
15	Sightseeing in Savannah	143
16	Discovery	153

CHAPTER 1

Savannah: An Introduction

IT IS ALMOST impossible to do a book about Savannah, for she is so very much a woman, infinitely old, tenderly young, mysterious, complicated, charming, a little evil, yet innocent, flirtatious and impossibly, incredibly, hauntingly beautiful.

When I discovered her, I fell instantly and quite madly in love. It was dusk when I first saw her, like a beautiful woman in a veil, poised, her lights, her spires, her fretted grillwork emerging through the twilight as I sped out of the marshes along Highway 17. It was Easter weekend—the radio was playing Handel's *Messiah* (Savannah, you are impossibly dramatic!)—and my sense of destiny, of having found a new and compelling region of the heart, was overwhelming.

The next day, Savannah shone in the morning light and the promise was fulfilled. It was April, and overblown crimson azaleas blazed in the historic squares. The trees were in new leaf round the noble statues of Oglethorpe, who founded the city, John Wesley, her spiritual mentor, and General Pulaski, a hero of the Revolution.

The tour I took that day was but the briefest introduction to the city—a hint—like a glance behind a fan. We saw the recently renovated Troup Square, in what had been one of the city's most dilapidated areas; a magnificent three-story mansion called the Juliette Gordon Low House, named for the founder of the Girl Scouts; the Telfair Museum, which houses the city's art treasures; and the ghost-ridden Jim Williams House, purged by an Episcopal bishop, site of a séance by Dame Sybil Leek. It is a seventeenth-century Rhode Island house with a gambrel roof, a house where organs blasted and beautiful mulatto ghosts sang until dawn, or so Jim Williams said.

We circled around the spectacular squares that Oglethorpe laid out, some for marketplaces, guardians now against urban blight, pollution and alienation; for here, on the fresh spring grass, emaciated winos mingled with crisp nursemaids, radiant children, and button-down businessmen in a happy meeting of the hearts. We drove down Victory Drive under an avenue of bearded oaks to Bonaventure Cemetery and roamed beneath towering azaleas amid the ancient crypts and tombs, by marble statues of beautiful children—"She was our angel"—past huge wrought-iron fenced crypts, the final resting place of whole families who had perished in the great yellow fever epidemics that had shaken the city, coming finally to a robed woman, an immutable stone angel like the patron saint of the city.

At luncheon, I met my cousin, New York appraiser Charlton Theus, at the Pirates' House, a favorite tourist spot in the beautifully restored Trustees' Garden. We sipped tall gin drinks in a convivial bar, dined on shrimp creole and French shrimp crepes, and I had a merry foretaste of an evening of revelry and adventure. But Charlton and I refused to be seduced. We broke away and drove through the white-hot afternoon past a shabby, heart-rending black ghetto to Fort Jackson, a recently restored fort built in the mid-nineteenth century and overlooking the Savannah River; there we prowled through the fortifications.

Inevitably, Savannah did seduce me on that trip. By dusk, when the offices at Factors Walk, once the heart of the cotton kingdom, were closing, the mood of the city changed dramatically. The ice was tinkling in the first gin drinks at the bar at the Sign of the White Hart, and an enormous black woman was playing away: "Hard-Hearted Hannah, the Vamp of Savannah, Ga." Another round? Who could resist? Oh yes, "Hard-Hearted Hannah," she seduced me that night. Somewhere, somehow, around the piano at the Sign of the White Hart, with revelers spilling out onto the street beneath the carriage lamps and the gang at the bar singing "Sweet Molly Malone." (Savannah's lineage is Irish, Jewish—Sephardic Jews of Spanish and Portuguese descent arrived only five months after the first English colonists—Anglo-Saxon, Scotch, and African, though she sometimes pretends to an impeccably pure Anglo-Saxon lineage.) Somehow, to the strains of Irish melodies and the singing around the bar, I wondered if any of us had been so clever before and if this moment, this pure moment of sweet camaraderie, would ever come again. Inevitably, and unforgettably, I was seduced.

Later, I was to learn more about her, about, for instance, the pollution of her air by paper mills run by the notorious Water Lords. And there is her neurotic side. Her rates of alcoholism and mental illness and suicide are climbing. She's having trouble adjusting to the twentieth century with all its shattering new problems—crime in the streets, for one—

problems she never faced before, for she had been protected, preserved since "the War."

But she'll make it. She is, after all, a lady, though she has had her lapses. The problems fade with the first sip of bourbon and branch water at dusk in the great, storied drawing rooms. The talk that once went back to the old days, to who married whom in pre-Revolution days and who fought what duel; and the endless recollections of the Civil War— THE War; there has never been any other—and the horrors of Reconstruction. All that is over now. Today the talk turns to the future, to the new industries coming in—clean industries like Grumman Aircraft—the restoration of once dilapidated neighborhoods, the shuttered rowhouses restored by men like banker Mills B. Lane; to new banks and new bridges, new hotels and the new Civic Center; to the restored houses, their impeccable lineage discreetly identified by Historic Savannah's wooden plaques; and now the restoration of the cobblestoned waterfront at historic Factors Walk. The talk is civilized, informed, forward-thinking. This is probably one of the most cultivated cities in the world.

To discover her is an adventure no less than a love affair. But, to know her, let us start, as a love affair should, with a discreet inquiry into her origins.

CHAPTER 2

Founding

LIKE MOST SOUTHERN gentlewomen, Savannah is inordinately proud of her lineage, which spans almost two and a half centuries and includes some of the most flamboyant, flawed and fascinating pioneers ever to set foot on American shores. Ancestor worship is Savannah's besetting sin, and the high point of her own peculiar calendar year is February 12, Founder's Day, when the sons and daughters of Savannah re-enact the birth of the city at a colorful ritual.

The ceremony, enacted with the city's high sense of pageantry, is simple and unvarying, but Savannahians like it that way. The good ship *Ann*, which brought its first settlers to America, was once depicted by the *Cruz del Sur*, an improbable Spanish galleon owned by banker-benefactor Mills B. Lane, of the C&S National Bank. In full sail, she used to steam down the Savannah River, flanked by an armada of power boats, yachts, and proud, noisy tugs.

The company on the *Ann* represent the first forty families to set foot on Savannah soil. Ironically, this impoverished group, a few of them taken from the cruel debtors' prisons of England, are depicted by members of the city's elite. The most coveted role is that of General James Edward Oglethorpe, founder of Savannah, a tall, striking military man turned humanitarian, who, as a member of Parliament, had investigated England's jails and found, among their many cruelties, none more harsh than the jailing of debtors, innocent of any crime except that of being slow to pay their bills. From this group, Oglethorpe, the visionary, dreamed of starting a new colony that would serve as a military buffer to the French at the west and the Spanish to the south at St. Augustine. Also, he hoped that its magnificent forest could be cleared for mulberry trees for the production of silk and arbors for the cultivation of wine grapes, the first step in solving England's eternal problem of the poor.

He seems to have given little thought to the qualifications of his colonists. There was only one gardener among them. The others were small tradesmen and shop keepers, chosen after interviews with the Trustees for the colony, a sturdy, robust group whose concept of the New World was that of a latter-day Garden of Eden. Their first view of Savannah, on February 12, 1733, seemed to confirm the wildest rumors of its beauty: vast expanses of golden marshes trembling under a brilliant sky, broken by forests of ancient, moss-bearded oaks and sapphire-blue streams and waterways. By nightfall, however, the colonists were slapping mosquitoes and complaining about the climate, the first in a long and bitter recital of their disillusionment that was to erupt finally in a lengthy plaint to the Trustees of the colony.

In retrospect, Oglethorpe's dream seems fantastic. He barred slavery, rum and lawyers. And he fully expected to turn a group of the indigent poor into crack militiamen and sophisticated agrarians in one of the first, and certainly among the boldest, ventures in man's long struggle against poverty and injustice.

On Yamacraw Bluff, he pitched his damask-lined tent and laid out the city, a town distinguished by its squares, the best-planned city in the United States, as most urban architects will tell you. Today, those squares are exquisitely planned oases in the city. A statue of Oglethorpe dominates Chippewa Square, an island blazing with azaleas and glazed with dogwood in the spring. This was Oglethorpe's town, and even today the city is a witness to his visionary genius.

Oglethorpe was to make two visits to England to recruit more settlers and beg for additional funds for the impoverished colony. In his absence, the "Malcontents," a group of disillusioned colonists, mounted an attack against him, finally issuing a bitter little pamphlet that was widely circulated in England. They accused the general of ruining the colony by his ban against slavery. Their neighbors to the north, in South Carolina, were flourishing agriculturalists, posing a continual source of envy to the impoverished Savannah colonists. They were infuriated by the ban on rum, which they insisted they needed in Savannah's sultry climate, and they opposed the "tail-male" system, which prevented wives and daughters from inheriting property. While tension mounted among the colonists, Oglethorpe devoted himself to the great military problem of protecting the colony from an invasion by the Spanish forces in Florida; he led one sea attack on St. Augustine, only to be soundly defeated. But he won a historic victory against the Spanish at Bloody Marsh on St. Simons Island, the site of Fort Frederica. Except for Fort William and Fort Andrew on Cumberland Island to the south, only

Oglethorpe's little army and his two ships stood between the American colonies and the Spanish at St. Augustine.

Oglethorpe's victory at Bloody Marsh was the decisive factor in preserving the colonies from Spanish dominion. It can be credited not only to the heroic stance of his militia, but also to a trick. He planted a letter on a defector boasting the strength of Oglethorpe's reserves, an army several times larger than his actual forces, the little band of zealots huddled in the marshes of St. Simons and a navy that did not exist. The credulous, marauding Spanish took the letter at face value and quickly decided to abandon their attack on Fort Frederica and return to St. Augustine. But Oglethorpe's historic victory was marred by the Malcontents. One of them, a military man who had moved in protest to Charleston, levied a court-martial against Oglethorpe. Though he was acquitted, on his return to England he watched the legalization of slavery and rum.

In August of 1749, with the threat of Spanish invasion thwarted, Georgia's founding fathers faced their first threat from the Indians. Mary Musgrove Bosomworth, the half-breed princess who had served as Oglethorpe's chief liaison with the Indians, led an attempt to capture the city. Historians believe she was deeply influenced by her third husband, Thomas Bosomworth, an Episcopal priest who never held a pulpit. Mary and Thomas induced a hundred Creek chieftains and warriors to rally in Savannah to support her claim to the coastal lands. Savannah, fearing a full-scale Indian attack, called out the militia, headed by Noble Jones and supported by a party of mounted men headed by quartermaster John Milledge.

The Indians entered Savannah in a long procession, headed by Mary, who was flanked by her husband and her cousin, Chief Malatchee. A report had circulated in the colony that the Indians had already beheaded William Stephens, Oglethorpe's overseer of the colony. Rumors crackled and tempers flared. Wrote one colonist: "Our inhabitants were so enraged that it was with the greatest difficulty they could be prevented firing on them and had not the members of the Board stood before the Indians til they were inclined to disperse it was feared the consequence would have been fatal."

Savannah's long history of seducing her captors originated with the great Indian encounter. The Indians were well received by Savannah's fathers, who persuaded them to disperse and join them for "a friendly glass of wine" at a tavern. As the evening's revelry began, Mary entered the room "like a mad and frantic woman," running in among them, "endeavoring all she could to irritate the Indians afresh," threatening the destruction of the colony by Indians under her influence. Mary was finally quieted by brute force and sentenced to the guardhouse for the night.

The following day, the Indians gathered in front of the courthouse to receive gifts from Savannah's leaders. Pacified, they were ready to return home, a prospect that made Chief Malatchee so angry that at least one witness reported he was foaming at the mouth. He was taken back to the tavern again, where he was soon mollified. Once again, Mary rushed in to stake her claim. "Spirited up with liquor, drunk with passion and disappointed in her views," she declared herself Empress and Queen of the Upper and Lower Creeks. She was advised to go home and go to bed, but the outraged Mary stirred the latent loyalty of Malatchee, who became once more incensed. Fearing an outbreak of violence, the peace officers removed Mary to a private room in the guardhouse. The revelry continued in a fine glow of Spanish rum that lasted "till dawn." By morning, the Indians had promised to leave the city. Savannah supplied them with provisions for the long journey home. A few days later they returned, complaining of the heavy rains which forced them to camp out. Provisions were dispersed and again they left, the final parting, which presaged their long and tragic exodus from their native land.

Mary was finally paid for her work as an interpreter. Her claim to the coastal islands was honored by the gift of St. Catherine's Island, where she lived out the rest of her life. Eventually, the Indians were given the hunting islands of Ossabaw, Sapelo and St. Catherine's.

While Mary lost an Indian kingdom, John Wesley lost his bid for spiritual superiority among the early settlers. As minister to Savannah, he also traveled to Frederica, where he met with a cold reception. A gnarled and bearded giant of an oak overlooking the Frederica River at the Methodist Camp Ground, Epworth-by-the-Sea, is pointed out now as the tree under which Wesley stood to preach the gospel to the Indians. But it is doubtful that any Indian was ever converted to Christianity by John Wesley. Certainly, during his sojourn at Frederica, he managed thoroughly to alienate himself from the shopkeepers and tradesmen of the colony there. He held morning service at five, afternoon service at three, and a Communion service at four. One of his Frederica communicants complained that "Wesley went from house to house exhorting the inhabitants to virtue and religion." When he left, full of bitterness and disillusionment with the Indians and the colonists, there were few regrets among the colonists.

It was in Savannah that Wesley made his most powerful enemies. His affairs there reached a climax when he refused Communion to a newly married maiden with whom he was purported to be in love. Her uncle was Thomas Causton, the storekeeper of Savannah, a man of some affluence and power. Wesley's romance with Miss Hopkey, if it was a romance, began on shipboard during a week-long voyage from Frederica to Savannah. On his return, the lovely Miss Hopkey went every morning to study French under the Reverend Mr. Wesley. He is said to have told her he'd like to spend the rest of his life with her, but he seems to have made no serious offer of marriage. Disappointed, she went to South Carolina to be married to young William Williamson by a priest notorious for conducting marriages without publishing the banns or issuing a license. Outraged, Wesley journeyed to South Carolina to reprimand the priest who had married them. Wesley was assured by the Reverend Alexander Garden, the Bishop of London's Commissary for South Carolina, and the other Anglican clergy of the colony, that they would marry no Georgians without a request by letter from Wesley. Wesley also took out his ire on Thomas Causton, accusing him of "giving short measure" at the store. Causton dealt patiently with Wesley until the ill-starred Sunday when he refused Communion to Sophey Williamson. "Savannah was electrified," wrote one of the family members. The following day, constable Noble Jones, a leading power in the colony, served a warrant on Wesley, in which Williamson demanded one thousand dollars damages for defaming Sophey by refusing to administer the Lord's Supper to her "in public worship" without cause. Wesley told magistrates Henry Parker and Thomas Christie that it was an ecclesiastical matter in which they had no right to interrogate him. Wrote one of the Trustees, the Earl of Egmont: "It appears to me that he [Wesley] was in love with Mrs. Williamson before she married and has acted indiscreetly with respect to her which is a great misfortune to us for nothing is more difficult than to find a minister to go to Georgia who has any virtue and reputation."

John Wesley never came to trial on the charge of defamation of character on the ten counts found against him by the grand jury. He asked trial in several courts, but it was always postponed, apparently at Causton's instigation. Realizing the danger of his position, he left Georgia after evening services on the night of December 2, 1737. Later he was to write: "Being now only a prisoner at large in a place where I knew by experience every day would give fresh opportunity to procure evidence of words I never said and actions I never did, I saw clearly the hour was come for me to fly for my life, leaving this place as soon as evening prayers were over, about 8 o'clock, the tide then serving. I shook off the dust of my feet and left Georgia after having preached the gospel there with much weakness indeed and many infirmities and nearly nine months! Oh that thou hadst known, at least in this thy day, the things which make for thy peace."

Journeying to Beaufort, he was lost for days in the woods and finally arrived in Charleston. From there he sailed for England, a deeply troubled man. It was a rough crossing, but in those days aboard ship he was to have the change of heart that presaged the birth of Methodism. Later he was to write: "It is now two years and almost four months since I left my native country in order to teach the Georgia Indians the nature of Christianity. But what have I learned myself in the meantime? Why, what I the least of all suspected, that I who went to America to convert others was never myself converted to God."

CHAPTER 3

The Revolution

THE REVOLUTION TOOK a heavy toll on Savannah. She was first besieged by the British, and later was the scene of the bloodiest battle of the war, when the French and the Americans tried to recapture her. Most buildings in the city were damaged by gunfire, and the women and children suffered mercilessly. The heroes of the tragic besiegement are still revered, with magnificent statues erected in their memory. The Revolution still burns in the hearts of many of the townspeople.

When the Stamp Act was first passed, in 1765, requiring stamps on all paper used for marriage certificates, deeds, records, contracts, notes, bonds or any legal purposes, the Savannah rebels organized for resistance, calling themselves the Liberty Boys, a name already in use by the other twelve colonies. The Stamp Act was first published in Georgia on October 31, a day of public celebration for the ascension of George III to the throne of the British empire five years earlier. The Liberty Boys celebrated by hanging a stamp officer in effigy. The first stamps arrived on December 5, 1765, but the British were so afraid the Liberty Boys would seize them that they had a guard of forty men protecting the dock hands while they were unloaded and put into the king's store. Royal Governor James Wright later had them moved to Fort George, on Cockspur Island, for safekeeping. The stamps were finally returned to England, but not before an effigy of Governor Wright holding a stamped sheet in his hand was paraded through the streets and burned.

During the celebration of Guy Fawkes Day that year, some sailors from the ships in the harbor joined in the holiday spirit of opposition by performing a rough drama of a mock beating of a stamp master. At MacHenry's tavern, they actually hanged the poor sailor acting the unpopular part—fortunately the rope was attached to his chest as well as his neck.

Tempers flared. The Stamp Act was the main topic of conversation everywhere. James Habersham, threatened with violence, hid for a while in the home of his friend Governor Wright, who called the Liberty Boys the Sons of Licentiousness.

After the Stamp Act was repealed, the Townshend Acts were passed, taxing all glass, lead, paper and tea imported into the colony. At a protest meeting in 1769, the Georgia Liberty Boys, following the lead of the other colonists, agreed to buy no English goods, including slaves, and they avidly rallied around the revolutionary cause after the Boston Tea Party in 1773.

Peter Tondee's tavern was the meeting place of the Liberty Boys. As a boy, Tondee had come to Savannah from, it is thought, Switzerland, and when his parents died, he became one of the first children to live in Bethesda Orphanage. He

The statue of General James Edward Oglethorpe, founder of Savannah in 1733, stands in Chippewa Square.

The Pirates' House, *ca.* 1832–50, now a restaurant in Trustees' Garden, was a seamen's inn built on the site of the first experimental garden in America, started in 1733.

The grave of Button Gwinnett, in Colonial Cemetery. Gwinnett was one of Georgia's representatives at the Second Continental Congress and signed the Declaration of Independence. In 1777 he died of wounds received in a duel.

The Graham vault, where at one time two Revolutionary War heroes were buried, Lieutenant Colonel John Maitland and Major General Nathanael Greene. The remains of General Greene were subsequently reinterred elsewhere.

The fountain, built in 1858, in Forsyth Park.

Wright Square, 1733, where stands a monument to William Washington Gordon, founder of the Central of Georgia Railroad (left); and Monterey Square, with its monument to Revolutionary War hero General Casimir Pulaski.

The Old Pink House, *ca.* 1789, one of Savannah's few remaining 18th-century houses, now a restaurant and tavern. Built by James Habersham, Jr., it became, in 1812, the first bank incorporated in Georgia.

The Hampton-Lillibridge House, on St. Julian Street, constructed in 1796 by a Rhode Island planter and known as the "ghost house" or the Jim Williams house. Ghosts once sang and danced there till dawn.

Historic Factors Walk, the heart of the cotton kingdom, where cotton brokers presided over the commerce that created the romantic Old South.

was an ardent revolutionary who encouraged the Liberty Boys and presided over the historic meeting in which they resolved to send six hundred barrels of rice and all the cash they could raise to Boston.

The loyalists were holding their meetings, too. Georgia was a divided colony. There were no compromises between the Liberty Party and the king. Families were bitterly divided. Some of the most notable clans in the colony were involved, including the Houstouns, the Gibbonses and the Farleys. Dr. Noble Jones, of Wormsloe Plantation, who had sailed with Oglethorpe on the *Ann* and quickly become a leading power in the new colony, was opposed by his own son, Dr. Noble Wimberly Jones, Speaker of the Commons House of Assembly; and James Habersham, acting as governor of the province, died in New Jersey, heartsick, after his sons, James and Joseph, and a nephew, Joseph Clay, assumed leadership in the Georgia Liberty Party.

Habersham had written to London on April 7, 1775, "The people on this Continent are generally almost in a state of madness and Desperation and should conciliating measures not take place on your side, I know not what may be the Consequences, I fear an open rebellion against the parent State and consequently amongst ourselves. . . . I must and do upon every occasion declare that I would not chuse to live here longer than we are in a State of proper Subordination to, and under the protection of, Great Britain. . . . May God give your Senators Wisdom to do it and heal this Breach; otherwise I cannot think of this event but with Horror and Grief. Father against Son and Son against Father and nearest relatives and Friends combating with each other. I may Perhaps say with Truth, cutting each others throats, dreadful to think of much less to experience."

The Liberty Boys, led by Noble W. Jones, Joseph Habersham and Edward Telfair, celebrated the news of the Battle of Lexington by breaking into the public powder magazine on May 11 and stealing five thousand pounds of gunpowder, which they sent, secreted in a shipment of rice along with some cash, to Boston, where the gunpowder was said to have been used at the Battle of Bunker Hill.

Wrote the sorrowing James Habersham: "I am greatly distressed about the bloody news we hear from the Northward and I am afraid there is now an end to all Reconciliation unless the blessed God by some extraordinary Interposition should bring it about, which I most humbly pray he may do—I think from this Event may be dated the almost ruin of Great Britain and this very flourishing Continent."

A reward of 150 pounds was offered for the arrest of the leaders, but no arrests were made; public sympathy was with the Liberty Boys. It was also with them when, on the king's birthday, the cannons placed on the river bluff to be fired in his honor were spiked and rolled down the bluff. That was on June 4. The following day, the Liberty Boys erected a liberty pole in front of Tondee's tavern and, two weeks later, elected a Council of Safety and raised their new flag to the top of the liberty pole.

The second Provincial Congress was held at Tondee's tavern on July 4, 1775, attended by one hundred delegates from all over the colony, who petitioned the king to change the laws Parliament had made against the Congress and made a public pronouncement to the people of Georgia that a civil war had begun. Archibald Bulloch was named president and George Walton was appointed secretary.

"The new government had no constitution, no sanction from the king and existed only with the approval of the people it served," pointed out historians Ronald G. Killion and Charles T. Waller in *Georgia and the Revolution*. "Yet in defiance of that government Wright was helpless."

When Governor Wright tried but failed to convene the Assembly, and the Provincial Congress took over the courts and militia, Wright requested troops from Parliament to help him enforce the law, but the British Army was already besieged in Boston. Powerless, Governor Wright asked to be recalled, but he was ordered to stay in Georgia and try to maintain order.

Georgia's role in the Revolution was initiated in July 1775, when Joseph Habersham and Oliver Bowen were ordered by the Provincial Congress to capture a British vessel anchored off the coast. The Georgia party, aided by some South Carolina ships, seized nine hundred pounds of gunpowder, five hundred pounds of which they sent to the Continental Congress.

After this, the Continental Congress recruited a battalion of 236 men under Colonel Lachlan McIntosh, of Darien, to defend Georgia. McIntosh had no delusions either about the difficulty of defending the seacoast or of its attractiveness to the British. In a letter to George Washington, he wrote: ". . . Our fine harbors make the security of this colony, though weak in itself, of the utmost consequence to the whole continent of America; and we have every reason to think our enemies intend to make it a place of general rendezvous and supplies."

The situation came to a head in January 1776, when three English war vessels anchored off Tybee to obtain supplies. Fearful that Governor Wright might order them to attack, the Council of Safety placed him under arrest. Ironically, it was Joseph Habersham who entered the mansion and allowed the beleaguered Wright to stay on in the mansion when he gave his word of honor not to communicate with the war vessels. Wright finally escaped, fleeing to Bonaventure Plantation, home of his friend John Mullryne, who had him transported to the English ship *Scarborough*. The English ships, having waited a month for supplies, captured a fleet of rice boats, and the Georgia Liberty Boys, after trying to negotiate for their return, sought help from the Carolina Militia, who boarded some of the boats and set fire to them. For Savannah, the war had finally begun.

But the colony had first to forge itself into a state. Under the leadership of President Archibald Bulloch, a constitution was written in February 1777, guaranteeing freedom of religion and the press, trial by jury and free schools in every county. The vote was limited to white Protestants, twenty-one years old and over, landowners who had lived in Georgia for at least twelve months.

The Liberty Party was in command. Representatives were sent to the Second Continental Congress, and the Declaration of Independence was signed by three of them: Button Gwinnett, Lyman Hall and George Walton. It was read to the roar of cannon in Savannah's squares, and an effigy of George III was dragged through the city streets and buried in a mock funeral.

The Liberty Boys were ready for action. General Robert Howe, who commanded the Southern Army, had his troops quartered in the port city of Sunbury in the fall of 1788, when he heard that the British planned to converge on Savannah from the sea, from the north and from Florida. The Scopholites, Tory defectors from South Carolina who had rallied in Florida, joined the British regulars and began their march up the coast, backed by five hundred men in a fleet of ships commanded by Colonel L. V. Fuser. They were to converge on Savannah with a British force of two thousand men sailing from New York under Colonel Archibald Campbell.

After a skirmish at Midway with the Florida forces, a deserter from the British ship *Neptune* reported to Governor Houstoun that Savannah, then unprotected, was to be attacked by Colonel Campbell, who was already sailing south from New York. When General Robert Howe was informed, he quickly abandoned Fort Morris at Sunbury and set out for Savannah with six hundred men.

When he reached the city, the first of Colonel Campbell's ships was already anchored in the Savannah River. There were two roads that led from Thunderbolt to Savannah, one a private road that crossed the marshes, which Howe ignored, deciding to guard the public road. This turned out to be a tragic mistake. The British learned of the marsh road from an old Negro man, Quamino Dolly, whom they hired as a guide. The road led them to the rear of the Savannah troops, while the British artillery stationed themselves in a field in front of the American forces. The rebels, besieged from both the front and the rear, fled and many drowned or were captured when they tried to cross Musgrove Creek. General Howe retreated to Cherokee Hill, eight miles from Savannah, and called for replacements, but Colonel Lane refused to leave his command at Sunbury, and Howe's fresh troops consisted of twenty men from South Carolina. In abject defeat he retreated to South Carolina, and Savannah was securely locked in British control.

There was one act of heroism Savannah has never forgotten. After the British took Ebenezer, the Salzburger Lutheran settlement north of Savannah, they marched their prisoners back to Savannah. When the guards paused at a spring to assuage their thirst, they put down their guns and rested, leaving only two men to guard the Ebenezer prisoners. Sergeant William Jasper and a Sergeant Newton, who had been awaiting the Salzburgers' arrival at the spring, shot the two guards and gathered up all their muskets and, with the aid of the released prisoners, captured the remainder of the British party. Jasper is still revered by Savannahians, who have erected a statue to him in one of the city squares.

Savannah was to have but one more chance to fight for her life. In September of 1779, forty-two French ships anchored off Tybee Beach with four thousand land troops aboard. The fleet was led by Count Charles-Henri d'Estaing, an ambitious Frenchman who had come to join the Americans in their struggle for liberty. The scattered rebel forces converged on Savannah at the urgent request of General Benjamin Lincoln, who called on every patriot in South Carolina and Georgia for help.

D'Estaing's troops were well supplied and well equipped. If they had stormed the city on their arrival, they would easily have taken Savannah from the British. But when D'Estaing demanded a surrender from General Augustin Prevost, then in control of the city, he allowed him several days to make his reply. These precious days of delay were to change the whole course of the Revolution. Prevost used them to repair his defenses and to send for reinforcements. When he received eight hundred regulars from Beaufort, under the command of Lieutenant Colonel John Maitland, he refused the surrender terms. When General Lincoln heard of the French threat, he immediately dispatched his South Carolina Continentals down the coast to Savannah to help in the city's defense. He was accompanied by General Casimir Pulaski and his cavalry.

Pulaski, a Polish nobleman, was a general in the American Army. A man without a country, he had left Poland when it was taken over by Russia, and gone to France, where he was enlisted under the auspices of Siles Deane and Benjamin Franklin to aid the American fight for freedom. Dashing and flamboyant, he was known throughout the colonies for his heroism, and his beautifully equipped cavalry was the most famous in the new nation.

It was in sharp contrast to the forces of General Lachlan McIntosh, who arrived from Augusta, and the forces from South Carolina and Virginia, who, for the most part, were dressed in homespuns and worn moccasins padded with Spanish moss. The British forces numbered a scant one thousand troops to provide a defense of the town.

On the 15th of September, D'Estaing, with two thousand Frenchmen, camped four miles out of Savannah. The men foraged for food as they marched, for provisions were running low. D'Estaing had delayed his attack to wait for Lincoln's troops to cross the Savannah River. There were jealousies and antagonisms among his own troops, and on shipboard, where rations had dwindled to two-year-old bread, the men were stricken with scurvy and, according to historians Clifford S. Capps and Eugenia Burney, in *Georgia, A Colonial History*, thirty-five dead men a day were buried at sea. The delay was to prove disastrous.

D'Estaing decided that an assault would prove futile and vowed to lay siege to Savannah. The allies launched their bombardment on the night of September 23 and, in a week, succeeded in damaging many buildings in Savannah. Though the Frenchmen, almost literally starving to death, wanted to retreat, D'Estaing insisted on an attack. General Lincoln agreed, as did General Pulaski, whose own plans were ignored. On October 9, D'Estaing met the rebel forces on the battlefield, charging to a drummer's beat, before all his troops had arrived. The vanguard attacked, but without reinforcements they were beaten back, and D'Estaing, wounded two times, couldn't rally his troops into a battle that meant certain death.

The heroic Pulaski, astride a black charger, led the attack, dashing ahead of his troops into the fire, rallying them to attack. At Spring Hill, scene of the heaviest fighting, he was hit by a blast of grapeshot and fell, mortally wounded. A few days later, he died on a hospital ship and was buried at sea. He is still revered as a hero by Savannahians, who have erected a statue to him also.

Baron Curt Von Stedingk planted the American flag at Spring Hill redoubt, but his troops, followed by General Lachlan McIntosh, soon retreated under British fire.

D'Estaing was found among the dead, still alive, and was taken by his men back to the ship. The battle had lasted an hour. Nearly a thousand men died in the conflict, one of the bloodiest of the American Revolution and possibly the one with the highest number of casualties. Most of the dead were Frenchmen. It was a crushing defeat. The French sailed back to the West Indies, from whence they had come. The Americans retreated to South Carolina. And the British continued to hold Savannah for three years, not evacuating until the summer of 1782. If the French and the Americans had won, the Revolution might have ended years sooner.

CHAPTER 4

The Code Duello

THE CODE DUELLO WAS ALREADY outlawed in England when Oglethorpe brought the first settlers to Georgia. But from the inception of the colony, the violence of the frontier was tempered by the infinitely mysterious and romantic landscape of golden marshes, dazzling blue estuaries and forests of moss-veiled oaks. Thus the bitter clashes that erupted in street or barroom brawls in the west found their expression in Savannah in duels, impassioned yet rigidly patterned by the rawest settlers according to the intricate code evolved by their aristocratic overlords.

The first recorded duel in Georgia occurred in May of 1741 between two of Oglethorpe's officers quartered at St. Simons Island. A Captain Norberry and a Captain Desbrisy clashed in what had begun as a wine fest, reconciled, quarreled again and drew swords, and Norberry, three wounds in his side, died instantly. But Captain Desbrisy went on to a heroic career, under Oglethorpe's leadership, as commander of a privateer, an officer renowned for his courage and daring who led the capture of Fort St. Francis from the Spaniards and headed the little force that held off the Spaniards when they sailed out to attack Oglethorpe's retreating forces after his ill-starred expedition against St. Augustine.

Oglethorpe's stance on dueling was never stated, though in his later years, living quietly and graciously among the London intelligentsia, he recounted to Samuel Johnson, Boswell and the poet Goldsmith at dinner one night how he met his first challenge when, at fifteen, serving under Prince Eugene of Savoy, the prince "took up a glass of wine and by a fillip made some of it fly in Oglethorpe's face," Boswell recounts. Oglethorpe, quickly considering the stigma of cowardice and the bitter result of any challenge, merely smiled and, in high good humor, replied, "*Mon Prince*, that's a good joke: but we do it much better in England," and threw a full glass of wine in the prince's face. This was Oglethorpe's only comment on Samuel Johnson's pronouncement, recorded by Boswell, that "a man may shoot the man who invades his character. As he may shoot him who attempts to break into his house."

Certainly in Georgia the brief and summary trial of Desbrisy on a manslaughter charge and his appointment as privateer dignified the code by Oglethorpe's implicit approval, and it became firmly implanted in the life of the colony.

As Savannah grew, took its stand against the British in the Revolution and the War of 1812, went on to become a port city rivaling Charleston and the queen city of the cotton kingdom, the code duello became the accepted way of handling disputes of every sort—property, personal injury, slander, a lady's virtue and, above all honor. It was at the very heart of the Savannah mystique, the dramatic moral assertion of a people given to trigger-tempered violence and the most exquisite gentility, of noble, bombastic, wine-flushed oratory and the basest and most insidious slander, of fierce righteousness and cruel vengeance—a flamboyant people, who forged out of the chaos of the times their own law and order.

The code became a sacred ritual, a dance of death, a drama replete with unflinching principals, heroic, foolhardy seconds scrupulously enforcing the unwritten rules, the attending surgeons and, waiting in the wings, the audience—the lusty, hot-blooded comrades in the taverns and regimental camps, the anguished mothers, wives and sweethearts wringing scented lace handkerchiefs behind shuttered windows. And there were the city fathers, impotent after their pleas for reconciliation; the press, standing by, reporting little but the death notices and funeral arrangements, to spare the grieving families; and finally, the clergy, helpless in the face of a code more powerful than the laws of God and man, a code uniquely sacred to a people, peasants and aristocrats alike, who had, as the years passed, embellished it with the feudal trappings and chivalric gallantry of Arthurian legend.

In retrospect, the fine aura of romantic fantasy is dimmed by a careful perusal of the facts, documented most scrupulously and accurately by historian Thomas Gamble in his little book *Savannah Duels and Duellists*. Most of Savannah's duels were neither very heroic nor historic, but their luster lingers among the old aristocracy, and their merits are debated still among the "well-connected" families of the coast.

The first significant duel of the Revolution between American officers was fought near Savannah in Governor Sir James Wright's meadow, attracting nationwide attention to the city and making it, overnight, a symbol of the high drama of the code.

The principals were Button Gwinnett, a signer of the Declaration of Independence, and General Lachlan McIntosh, a descendant of the Highlanders who had settled Darien under Oglethorpe's command, a courageous, fiercely independent man, commander of the Georgia Continental Line in the early days of the Revolution. Although, in the coastal custom, the challenge was precipitated by a charge of slander, the two men, both ambitious, had long been bitter political rivals.

Gwinnett, who had pursued a merchant's career in Bristol, England, had moved on to Charleston and then, in 1765, to Savannah. He retired after three years to St. Catherine's Island, purchasing his land from the fabled Bosomworths, and settled into the life of a coastal planter. In 1776 he was elected a delegate from St. John's Parish to the Provincial Congress and was sent on as a delegate to the Congress at Philadelphia, where he emerged as an ardent advocate of the Jeffersonian ideal and signed the Declaration of Independence.

By then fully committed to the colonial stance against England, he became a member of the Georgia Council of Safety and helped father the Georgia State Constitution of 1777. At the death of President Archibald Bulloch, Gwinnett was appointed by the council as commander-in-chief of Georgia and ordered by the executive council to march into Florida "with a competent force of Militia and Volunteers, erect the American standard and proclaim protection and security of person and property to all who would take the oath of allegiance," reports Gamble.

Florida, still under the dominion of Spain, had fought many a bloody battle with the British, but it had not yet allied itself to the colonies to the north. It was a rare plum, both to the emerging union statesmen and the military and to Lachlan McIntosh, who, as a brigadier general, expected to lead Georgia's military forces into Florida. But Gwinnett intervened and took over the foray himself, sending Colonel Baker and his military forces by land and Colonel Elbert with the Continentals by sea to a rendezvous on the St. John's River—an expedition quickly and disastrously repelled by the Spaniards, "conceived in ambition, planned without due caution and sadly marred in execution," as one historian put it.

When the new assembly met, Gwinnett was ignominiously dismissed. The jubilant McIntosh denounced him as a scoundrel and lying rascal before the executive Council, and Gwinnett immediately challenged him to "mortal combat."

In the hot, languid dawn of Friday, May 16, 1777, the two men met, faced each other at four paces and fired. Each was wounded in the thigh. According to Dr. Lyman Hall, a Liberty County signer of the Declaration of Independence who wrote to still another signer, in Philadelphia, explaining the incident: "Mr. Gwinnett's thigh broke so that he fell. On wh'h 'tis said the General asked him if he chose to take another shot. Was answered Yes, if they would help him up (or words nearly the same). The seconds interposed.

"By Monday, Gwinnett was dead," Hall mourned. "O Liberty why do you suffer so many of your faithful sons, your warmest Votaries, to fall at your shrine? Alas, my Friend, my Friend. Excuse me, Doctor Sir, the man was VALUABLE so attached to the Liberty of this State and Continent that his whole Attention, Influence and Interest centered in it and seemed rooted to it. He left a Mournful Widow and Daugr. and I may say the Friends of Liberty on a whole Continent to deplore his fall."

Although Savannah's law officers had chosen to ignore

the duel, McIntosh surrendered to the civil authorities, gave bond, was indicted, tried and acquitted. But the death had left deep wounds. On the advice of both his friends and enemies, he transferred to the northern forces and served so valiantly under Washington that the general commended him in a letter to the Continental Congress. Returning south a hero, he was second in command of the American forces when the British attacked Savannah in 1779 and was finally imprisoned by the British when General Lincoln surrendered at Charleston. The war over, he resided briefly in Virginia, but Savannah was his home, and ultimately he returned there to die, in February of 1806. McIntosh County bears his family's name; Gwinnett County honors the master of St. Catherine's. Georgia seldom dishonored her duelists.

During the incendiary days of the Revolution, Savannah was renowned for the drama of her duels, recorded today on the blurred tombstones of Colonial Cemetery in the city's heart. But today James Jackson is remembered as chief of Savannah duelists.

Jackson came to Georgia from England in 1772 at the age of fifteen, on fire with the patriots' cause; and distinguished himself in battles with the British from old Midway Church to Cowpens, where he won the rank of major, with a reputation for unusual courage and military skill. Today he is remembered as a revolutionary hero, organizer and leader of the Jeffersonian party in Georgia, United States senator, and nullifier of the sale of the western empire of Georgia to speculating land companies. But every victory was won inevitably with a battle of blood, a contest on "the field of honor."

His first adversary was Lieutenant Governor George Wells. The immediate cause of the duel is lost in history, but their animosity went back to the first patriots' meeting at

Tondee's tavern on August 10, 1774, where Wells, a wealthy planter of Jefferson County, countered Jackson's revolutionary stance with a protest that it "reflected improperly upon the King and Parliament."

By June of 1776, Wells had obviously given up hope of a just peace with Britain and was appointed by the Council of Safety a justice of the peace for St. Paul's Parish. His career was marred by scandal, but again the details are lost in history. When the patriots refugeed to Augusta, he was elected colonel of the Lower Battalion of the Augusta District only to be "accused of heinous crimes" which he never refuted and which cost him his post. But by February 1780 he was elected to a seat in the Continental Congress and became acting governor of Georgia.

It was Jackson who issued the challenge, describing Wells as "governed by jealousy, inordinate ambition and a desire for power and place." Where they met is not known. History records that, in a simple agreement to fight out their differences, the two men met, parted by but a few paces. Wells was instantly killed, and Jackson, wounded in both knees, survived to become the first American soldier to enter Savannah on July 12, 1782, when the British evacuated and the patriots took over the city. It was to him that General Wayne gave the key to the city.

Jackson's next opponent was the noted Savannah lawyer Thomas Gibbons. Defending his post as representative to the First Congress in the First Georgia District against General "Mad Anthony" Wayne, Jackson was defeated through the machinations of Gibbons, whom he accused of falsifying the polls in Glynn and Effingham counties. Jackson contested his defeat before the House of Representatives in Washington, accusing Gibbons of "abominable corruption, leaving Chatham county to influence the electors of Effingham county and corrupt even the magistrates themselves."

Jackson's fiery oratory won wild applause in the House, but after a tie vote between himself and Wayne, both men declined to run and the post went to John Milledge, Jackson's friend and political lieutenant. Wayne later became commander-in-chief of the American Army and died a hero's death in a battle against the Indians in the Ohio territory. Gibbons, by then mayor of Savannah, met Jackson's accusations with a challenge, and the two men exchanged three shots, but neither was hit and they later became loyal friends.

Jackson's most notable victory, the repeal of the Yazoo land grant, made him many enemies, some of whom challenged him to duels and one who tried to assassinate him. At the request of the citizens of Savannah, Jackson had resigned from the United States Senate to win a seat in the Georgia Legislature and lead the struggle against the Yazoo Act. Passed by a "corrupted Legislature," the Act had allowed a group of northern speculators to buy at one and a half cents an acre some thirty-five million acres of land extending from the Chattahoochee River to the Mississippi and from the border of the Spanish territory on the Gulf to the border of Tennessee. The land was sold at enormous profit to unwary Northerners.

After the Legislature amended the Act under Jackson's leadership, the purchasers sought redress from Congress, where the issue was fought out for years and, finally, was settled after a history-making decision by the Supreme Court under Chief Justice John Marshall asserting the court's right to annul state laws passed in violation of the national Constitution.

Actually, the seeds of secession went back to the Yazoo

Fraud. Daniel Webster, then serving his first term in the House, fighting to see his defrauded New England constituents reimbursed, exulted over the victory of the Yazoo bill, unanimously supported by the Federalists but opposed with "great heat" by Georgians, Virginians and Carolinians.

Shortly after the victory, a group of Jackson's enemies, led by Robert Watkins of Augusta with a posse of his Yazoo friends, surrounded him as he was leaving the State Capitol at Louisville. Jackson defended himself "with my little Lucas stick." When it broke, he ordered Watkins "to take his ground." As Jackson fired, the gun was knocked from his hand and Watkins ran at him with a bayonet. Jackson threw him twice and was "beating him handsomely" when "a scoundrel by the name of Wood" rushed to defend Watkins, who then tried to gouge out Jackson's eyes—the most dishonorable of all offenses in the code. When repulsed, he drew another bayonet and stabbed the unarmed Jackson in the collarbone and ribs, and Jackson was saved only when a group of his friends rushed to his rescue.

After resisting a series of challenges from other Yazoo supporters for four years, Jackson, by then governor of the state, threatened once again by a renewal of the Yazoo Act, met Watkins three times in carefully ordered duels, finally wounding him so severely that the second intervened. According to one observer, "Jackson and Watkins conversed with great elegance and entire politeness on different matters, while the seconds were arranging the terms of the combat that within the next minute was expected to put an end to at least one of them." Ultimately, the wounds suffered in that final encounter cost Jackson his life, but not before the indomitable patriot had won an enviable reputation in the United States Senate. For years afterward, he was honored for his leadership in the Georgia Legislature's amendment of the Yazoo Act.

So deeply was the code entrenched in the Savannah mystique that men of the highest reputation feared to refuse a challenge on the slightest charge from the basest adversary for fear of the label of cowardice. A notable exception is General Nathanael Greene, whose heroism as Washington's commander-in-chief during the Revolution had been rewarded by a handsome estate near Savannah, Mulberry Grove, renowned today as the place where Eli Whitney, as tutor to Greene's children, invented the cotton gin.

Greene's challenger was Captain James Gunn, destined to become the mastermind of the Yazoo Fraud. A Virginia lawyer born in 1739, he had served as captain of the dragoons under General Wayne, helped regain Savannah from the British and, after the Revolution, made the city his residence.

He had nurtured a smoldering bitterness against Greene since 1782, when the general, then his commanding officer, subjected him to a court of inquiry. Gunn had sold a horse belonging to the Army without orders. Although the court exonerated Gunn, Greene took the matter to Congress, which supported him and reprimanded Gunn, who challenged the general soon after the war was won. Colonel James Jackson, later to become Gunn's bitter antagonist, issued the challenge, then quickly withdrew from the affair after Greene explained the matter, saying that, while "no man ever heard me use language that would disgrace a gentleman," he felt his act was "criminal and altogether unwarrantable," but he refrained from bringing Gunn before a court-martial and stripping him of his commission.

Still Gunn persisted, issuing a second challenge through Benjamin Fishbourne, a fellow revolutionary in the first regiment of Chatham County Militia. Greene again refused, contending that if a superior officer could be so held responsible for discipline of subordinate officers, all military discipline would be subverted.

Greene's was a courageous decision in a day when "to refuse satisfaction rendered one subject to the charge of cowardice—the unforgiveable sin—and to the probable loss of public esteem." It was not lightly made. To General Washington he wrote in anguish, "If I thought my honor and my reputation would suffer in the opinion of the world and more especially with the military gentlemen, I value life too little to hesitate a moment to accept the challenge."

From Mount Vernon, Washington immediately replied, ". . . Your honor and reputation will stand, not only perfectly acquitted for the non-acceptance of this challenge, but that your prudence and judgment would have been condemned by accepting it; because if a commanding officer is amenable to private calls for the discharge of his public duty, he has always a dagger at his heart. . . ."

Gunn—"violent, aggressive, overbearing," his friends described him—threatened Greene with a personal assault. The general's cool reply: "I always wear pistols and will defend myself."

But he was careful never to ride through town at dusk, and the intense heat of the noonday sun cost him the sunstroke from which he died in 1786, a year after Gunn's challenge. Gunn went on to become a United States senator, still a staunch defender of the Yazoo Fraud, and history last describes him striding through the streets of Augusta in broadcloth and a high beaver hat, cracking a whip at his Yazoo opponents.

The seething political antagonism between Federalist

and Republican factions that raged through the states after the Revolution erupted in the bloodiest and bitterest duels in Savannah. Explains Gamble: "The Federalists were damned as Tories, Royalists and Imperialists," while the Republicans were branded as "the red-capped guillotinists of property rights and intelligence and integrity."

A deadly undercurrent of malice and envy, hatred and slander and selfish antagonisms marred the infinite beauty of the "garden city," as foreign visitors often called it, and even its merriest moments of revelry could trigger a death-dealing duel.

Ironically, General David B. Mitchell, the man who as governor signed Georgia's first law against dueling on December 12, 1808, had himself killed one of Savannah's leading citizens, William Hunter, who had served as navy agent for Georgia under Jefferson. His resignation stirred speculation that he had "returned to Federalism as a first love." Although Mitchell was a native Scotsman, born in 1766, he had come to Savannah in 1783 to look after his uncle's property, went on to study law, and became a member of the legislature and a staunch opponent of the Yazoo Act. Though the Revolution was won before he came to the United States, he became so fierce a patriot that he declared before the legislature: "If I ever find it in my heart to forgive an old Tory his sins, I trust my God will never forgive mine."

Mitchell was mayor of Savannah when the duel took place, on August 23, 1802, in the Jewish cemetery. The cause of the conflict, indeed the duel itself, was discreetly ignored by the Savannah press. It was the New York *Daily Advertiser* which recorded the drama, the meeting at ten paces, the deadly advance of two paces after each shot—one, then another, then the fatal third, which pierced Hunter's heart, and later the funeral, "attended by the most respectable citizens of Savannah, by whom he was highly esteemed and respected."

A year later, on July 4, a day of parades and reviews, wining and dining, Hunter was toasted by his own troop of the light horse: "His virtues were rare, may his example be ever present and influential to us." At a nearby tavern, amid much revelry, Colonel Mitchell lifted his glass to "Thomas Jefferson. May that virtuous Republican statesman continue to deserve the title of 'man of the people.'"

Seven years later, on a frosty morning in the governor's office at Milledgeville, Mitchell signed the act making it unlawful to extend or accept a challenge on penalty of exclusion from the "right to hold any office of trust, honor or emolument in the State."

And yet, as Gamble reports, "neither before nor after was there a predominant sentiment to sustain prosecutions." Aaron Burr, after killing Hamilton in the duel of July 1, 1804, was given a hero's welcome in Georgia—a seventeen-gun salute at St. Mary's—and after a sojourn with Major Pierce Butler on St. Simons, was embraced with great fanfare by Savannah Republicans.

In the face of the law of 1809, the city's three newspapers continued to publish the most outrageous and incendiary personal attacks, blatant invitations to a challenge. Typical was John Moorehead's simple advertisement in the Savannah *Republican:* "I hold Francis H. Wellman a Liar, Coward and Poltroon."

More subtle were anonymous attacks such as this one that appeared in the old *Gazette:* "To deal in calumny accords with the lineaments of this gentleman's contracted phiz and phlegmatic constitution, the features of his countenance appear clouded with malignant passion; his soul is prone to false invective; and though the insidious smile should now and then relax the furrows in his brow, it bears no claim to benevolence."

Such attacks were frequently posted at the Vendue House, where the city hall now stands, where citizens gathered daily to read the sale of Negro slaves, plantation land, merchandise and schooners; rewards for runaway slaves; and malicious cartoons and slanderous attacks, crudely penned, that begged for a rebuttal on the dueling ground.

One of the few Savannahians who refused a challenge with no qualms was Israel K. Tefft, who, in 1824, was defeated by the "underhanded" methods of a newcomer, William Turner, in his bid to be sergeant of the Chatham Artillery. After he published his complaints at a company parade on Washington's birthday, Turner attacked him. Tefft trounced him thoroughly, and when Turner posted two challenges against him, Israel sagely and sardonically "declined the glorious pomp and circumstance of a duel" and went on to become a successful banker and a founder of the Georgia Historical Society in 1839, which he served as secretary until 1862. His collection of autographs from those prominent in literature, art and politics from all over the world was considered the most distinguished in the United States and so fascinated Swedish novelist Fredrika Bremer, taken not only by the autographs but their accompanying copperplate engravings and personal letters, that she declared him "the greatest autograph collector in the world."

As Savannah emerged as a major port and the reigning capital of the cotton kingdom, the plantation system, with all its feudal trappings, produced a dueling system that was, at its best, chivalric and sometimes gallant in the Arthurian tradition and, at its worst, the fatal encounters of arrogant, swaggering hotheads and fools.

Among scions of the aristocracy, almost anything could provoke a duel: a horse race, a toast to a New England politician, an anti-Irish song, an intimation of dishonesty, ingratitude, cheating at cards, a dispute over costs or politics (yes, almost always politics) or an allusion to a lady's honor.

In December 1826, a citizens meeting was called at the City Exchange to found the Savannah Anti-Duelling Association, for the "purpose of restraining and, if possible, suppressing the practice of duelling" by acting as reconciliators whenever an impending duel was brought to their attention. The president was Dr. George Jones, son of Dr. Noble Wimberly Jones, of Wormsloe Plantation, a man widely known as Savannah's first citizen, a former judge of the Supreme Court, a United States senator, and president of the Savannah Temperance Association.

The association continued to function as a moral force until 1837, but it seems to have produced little but eloquent oratory, most notable of which was the first anniversary meeting, attended by the Chatham Artillery in full regalia, at which attorney Matthew Hall McAllister denounced dueling as a "mouldering and decayed relic of chivalry," corrupted by Italian morals whose insidious effect upon the whole of Europe had engendered "deceit, exciting a feverish thirst for revenge and creating a strong disposition toward the coarsest licentiousness everywhere." But they also framed and passed the legislative act of December 19, 1828, requiring all civil and military officers appointed on and after July 1, 1829, to take an oath that they had not, since that date, been engaged in a duel.

But the code was too powerful for law. The hot-blooded

Savannahians continued to fight. The breeding places for dispute were race tracks and taverns, most notably the City Hotel, where the seasoned sailor Captain Wiltberger presided at the bar—"the rendezvous of the leading young men of the city and all the country between Savannah and the Florida line," as one journalist called it.

Though the cooler heads of the Anti-Duelling Association often tried to intervene, they were rarely successful. Commented an observer in Baltimore in 1847 in a little book, *The Code of Honor or the Thirty Nine Articles:* "Such laws [against duelling] . . . are evaded or trampled upon by the very Legislators who framed them. And when they ever were carried into effect, which popular feeling would render somewhat impracticable, duelling would not be prevented, because the practice of duelling is supported and encouraged by public sentiment and because that man who declines a fair and honorable challenge is branded as a coward."

Despite attacking the abuse of dueling, the author— "Southron," he called himself—voiced the view of most of his countrymen that "the duel is a sharp but salutary remedy for rude and offensive conduct, and its most inveterate opponents must admit that, wherever encouraged, it has produced at least a marked courtesy and polish of manners."

Yet the cold brutality of the code shocked many a foreign visitor, among them the noted English tragedian W. C. Macready, who on a January night in 1844, after playing to a crowded house, strolled down the bluff, enchanted by the great gnarled oaks and a starlit vista of marshland and river, when the ineffable beauty and romance of the Savannah night were shattered by an encounter with a hospitable stranger who invited him to his home for a glass of wine, to await a midnight duel between "two gentlemen of the bar,"

The Richardson-Owens-Thomas House, 1817, designed by William Jay.
The Bacon House on East State Street. Early-19th century.

Davenport House, 1820, Historic Savannah's first purchase and one of the country's finest Georgian buildings.

Interiors, the Green-Meldrim House, *ca.* 1840, where General Sherman stayed when his Union forces moved into Savannah on December 21, 1864. (Courtesy of the Library of Congress and the Historic Savannah Foundation, Inc.)

Fort Pulaski, on Cockspur Island, was expected to be Savannah's main defense in the Civil War. It was taken over by the Confederate Army in January of 1861, but in April it was captured by Union troops. (Aerial view courtesy of the Historic Savannah Foundation, Inc.)

On Orleans Square, the Champion-McAlpin-Fowlkes House, early-19th century. Its fine Greek Revival façade is shaded by now massive yew trees, each planted at the birth of a McAlpin son.

The Telfair Academy of Arts and Sciences, built by William Jay in 1820. Since 1875, Savannah's finest museum, noted for its interiors and its antique furniture.

The birthplace of Juliette Gordon Low, built 1819–21.

Detail, Telfair Academy.

Founder, the Girl Scouts of America.

The Waring House on West Taylor,. built in 1852. The Dutch look was added in a later remodeling.

The tower of the county jail.

on Hutchinson Island, across the river. To the incredulous Macready, the stranger explained that the legal authorities dared not interfere: the principals had too many friends among them, and the townspeople, maintaining with infinite discretion the secrecy of the encounter, were merely gathering on the bluff to hear the outcome, which would, of course, go unreported by the press. "My stomach felt sick with horror at the cold-blooded preparation for murder with which he acquainted me," Macready recalled.

In the decade before secession, the Chatham Club became the refuge of the young bloods. It was there, over billiards, cards and brandy, that the fate of the Union was endlessly debated in conflicts that often ended in challenges. This was the last desperate hour of the chivalric myth, the Arthurian fantasy, and conflicts that were once blatantly and violently resolved in full view of the city in the Jewish cemetery or at Fort Wayne on the waterfront were now fought at the more remote Screvens Ferry, just across the river, in South Carolina.

"One might think the very soil into which had already soaked the life blood of the impetuous would cry out against further sacrifice," wrote Gamble. Though these encounters were seldom formally reported except by the northern press, Savannahians knew the details almost before the stricken families, and gathered at the East Broad Street dock silent before the awesome drama of death, to watch the corpse-laden boat come slowly down the river to be received by the bereaved, who, true to the last ritual of the code, lifted their dead sons in their arms with faces "fixed as stone."

Seldom even did the tomb reveal the anguish wrought by the code to the families, the comrades, the regimental brothers of the dead. Rare are epithets like the inscription on the tomb of a poet's brother, James Wilde, who lies buried in Colonial Cemetery, Savannah's old burying ground.

This humble stone
Records the filial piety
Fraternal affection and manly virtues
of
James Wilde, Esquire
late District Paymaster in the Army of the U.S.
He fell in a Duel
on the 16th of January, 1815
by the hand of a man
who, a short time ago, would have been
friendless but for him
And expired instantly in his 22nd year
dying as he had lived:
With unshaken courage and unblemished reputation
By his untimely death the prop of a mother's age is broken;
The hope and consolation of sisters is destroyed
The pride of brothers humbled in the dust
And a whole Family, happy until then,
overwhelmed with affliction.

Even after the great bloodletting of the Civil War, amid the chaos of Reconstruction, the conflict between the old aristocracy and new radicals frequently erupted into duels, usually after heated debate in the local newspapers.

Savannah's last fatal duel was fought in 1870 over an issue almost as incendiary as politics: the competition among yachtsmen and the merits of their craft. The principals were Ludlow Cohen, a popular young businessman originally from Charleston, and Richard F. Aiken, a Darien rice planter twice his opponent's age—both ardent yachtsmen. Inordinately proud of their swift vessels, they were challenged to a race by a group of sportsmen gathered at Beaulieu and, stirred by the swift-racing breeze and a zestful audience, set sail immediately, with Aiken's son in charge of the stake boat stationed two miles from the starting point. Cohen's yacht plunged ahead and passed the stake boat ahead of Aiken's just as the breeze died out, and the race subsided into a drifting match back to Beaulieu. The sportsmen pleaded for a second match, but Cohen refused on the grounds that Aiken "is not a gentleman," accusing Aiken's son of moving the stake boat forward to give his father an unfair advantage. Aiken replied immediately with a written challenge. At dawn the next morning, under the ancient oaks of Bramptom Plantation, where the Savannah slaves had held their first worship service, the two men met at twelve paces. Four shots were exchanged although the code forbade more than two each, but neither man was hit. Asked by a friend if he was nervous, Aiken cockily tossed his pistol in the air, caught it by the end of the barrel, coolly faced his adversary, and for the fifth time, at the signal "fire," pulled the trigger. Cohen responded with the fatal shot and, after delivering himself over to Justice Isaac M. Marsh, faced a jury trial, but there was no indictment, and the newspapers, though reporting the encounter in detail, made no editorial comment against the code.

But public sentiment was finally and irrevocably aroused and, under the State Code of 1873, the issuing of a challenge was made punishable by six months imprisonment, and as for a fatal duel, "all parties, both principals and seconds," were charged with murder and, on conviction, sentenced to the death penalty.

Other challenges were issued, other duels were fought by

native Savannahians even as late as 1899, but as Gamble tells us, in the end it was not law or moral force or the extremes of tragedy that ended the code in Savannah.

It was the incisive wit of Joel Chandler Harris, creator of Uncle Remus, who as a young reporter on the Savannah *Morning News* recounted the murderous clashes between embattled Savannahians so drolly that the principals became a laughingstock. Among them was the "Roaring Lion, Colonel Gaulden of Liberty County, who went raging through the cobblestone streets of Savannah, after issuing an unanswered challenge to Walter Way, pursuing him with ringing oaths and a flourishing pistol all the way to Screvens Ferry, only to return, no bullet fired, to announce to the bemused press how savage would have been his vengeance against his cowardly adversary."

To Savannah, proudest of all cities, it was only ridicule that could devastate the sacred code as Cervantes had devastated a "ludicrously degenerated chivalry in his *Don Quixote*," as Gamble points out, "making it the target of satire and jeering laughter when occasion offered, against which no custom, no matter how time-honored, could long continue to exist."

CHAPTER 5

Of Slavery and the Wanderer

IRONICALLY, SAVANNAH, queen city of the only colony of the original thirteen to outlaw slavery, was destined to become, with the invention of the cotton gin there, the capital of the cotton kingdom, the teeming center of the slave trade and its most eloquent and impassioned defender.

It was the fiery-tongued city fathers of Savannah who for a century dictated the slave code, meted out punishment, and upheld with blazing moral conviction the civilizing force of "the great institution." And it was the dashing young scion of one of the city's most prominent families who smuggled the last shipload of slaves aboard the fabled ship *Wanderer* and delivered them to Jekyll Island, Georgia, fifty years after the slave trade had become legally abolished and on the very eve of "the War."

Although Oglethorpe had bitterly objected to the introduction of slavery to Georgia, the general was himself a member of the Royal African Company, which traded in slaves, and the owner of a plantation using slaves in South

Carolina. The motives of the Great Philanthropist were in this case not philanthropic. Slaves, he believed, were beyond the means of his original settlers. He was convinced they would encourage the habits of indolence that had first brought them to destitution, that they had no place in a colony devoted to the production of silk and wine, and were a positive danger to Georgia's precarious position as military buffer against the Spanish to the south and the French to the west.

Five years after the founding of Savannah, the pressure for slavery was so intense that the benighted Savannahians, unable to cultivate either mulberry trees or grape arbors in the sandy soil of the low country, petitioned the Trustees for Negroes. The petition was eloquently countered by the industrious Salzburgers at nearby Ebenezer, who insisted they could "easily gain bread and subsistence and lead a quiet and peaceful life in godliness and honesty." The Scotch at Darien, to the south, wrote, "It is shocking to human nature that any race of man and posterity be sentenced to perpetual slavery."

The petition denied, many planters abandoned their lands, and the Malcontents, in their tract *A True and Historical Narrative of the Colony of Georgia in America*, insisted that no white man could endure labor in the swampy fields of the coast without suffering "fluxes, tremors, vertigo, palsies" and a variety of painful and lingering nervous distempers which brought to many a "Cessation both from Work and Life."

Savannah was fighting for its life. By 1741, the population was approximately 2,025. Spurred by the charges of the Malcontents, Thomas Stephens humiliated his father, William Stephens, by pressing another petition, signed by 123 freeholders, to the King himself, who ordered an investigation of the Trustees by Parliament; but with Oglethorpe embroiled in the battle with Spain, the matter was dropped.

Slavery had its dangers. In the South Carolina insurrection of 1739, Georgians were pillaged and burned. In Savannah, the air was electric. Slaves, quite openly, were being purchased from South Carolina. "To the one thing needful" was the none too subtle toast in the taverns of the town, and by 1748, feeling was so inflammatory that even the Salzburgers gave in, the magistrates capitulated, and by 1749, George Whitefield, founder of Bethesda Orphanage, and James Habersham, most respected and benign of the city fathers, were able to convince the Trustees, by petition, of the desperate necessity of slavery and of "the moral good done the Negro by transporting him to a Christian land."

The crown capitulated. The long-awaited law of 1750, which fixed the ratio of male Negroes to one to every four whites, was sanctified by philanthropic overtones. Slaves were to be compelled to spend Sundays attending services conducted by a Protestant minister and to be taught the sanctity of marriage. Even for murder, Negroes were to be tried according to the laws of England, and, explicitly, slaveowners were, by a code of liberal laws, not allowed to abuse their "property."

With slavery came prosperity. Oglethorpe returned to England, the Trustees surrendered the charter to the crown, new settlers poured in, rice and indigo flourished, antislavery sentiment vanished, and the slave code was gradually toughened.

After the abortive Stono rebellion in South Carolina, blacks were deemed in 1770 "chattels, personal in the hands of their owners and possessors." They were rigidly patrolled, forbidden to travel the highroads in groups of more than seven unless accompanied by a white person, and forbidden to use firearms without a license from their masters; capital punishment and severe whippings were adopted from the South Carolina code. Stringent restrictions were also imposed upon the masters, and the teaching of a slave to read or write carried a far heavier penalty than to work one unduly. Even the teachings of the Bible, once so sacrosanct, were deemed dangerous. Only in Savannah were slaves, if properly licensed, permitted to sell or buy fruit, fish or garden stuff and work as porters, carters or fishermen. The invention of the cotton gin by Eli Whitney, New England-born tutor to the household at Mulberry Plantation, revolutionized Savannah's waning economy in the decade after 1793. Cotton became king, the plantation system flourished, and the heroic defenders of freedom became feudal lords who embraced the Platonic philosophy, that the inequality of man was fundamental to all social organizations and that slavery was supported by history, the Bible and economics.

On the great Savannah plantations that grew up during this period, for instance the Hermitage, still known for its "Savannah grey" brick, slaves were well treated.

However, the piety that had tempered the introduction of slavery to Georgia was suddenly reversed. The plantation owners believed the teachings of Christianity threatened the whole system unless carefully interpreted. Savannahians imprisoned George Liele, a former slave, whose kindly master had allowed him to preach to the blacks along the Savannah River and at Yamacraw. Before he escaped to Jamaica, he baptized a convert, Andrew Bryan, and Bryan's wife, Hannah, and twenty of the slaves at Brampton Plantation, with his master's blessing. But when Bryan brought his doctrine to

Savannah, he was publicly flogged. Lacerated and bleeding, the whip still lashing his back, Bryan cried out to his persecutors that he rejoiced not only to be whipped but would gladly "suffer death for the cause of Jesus Christ." When he and his brother were jailed for inciting an insurrection, his master intervened and he returned to Brampton to his growing flock to pray for those who flogged him.

When word got back to Savannah, his persecutors, stunned and moved, agreed that Andrew should be granted his freedom and allowed to preach in Savannah. With the help of Lachlan McIntosh, who filed an eloquent petition in Andrew's behalf, a lot on Bryan Street was deeded to "Free Andrew" June 1, 1790. Here he and his followers built the First African Baptist Church, the first Negro church in the United States. Andrew, tall, white-haired, full of dignity, lived to become one of Savannah's most respected and beloved citizens. Strangely, Andrew never took a stand against slavery.

But, then, slaves were, according to visitors like the British traveler Basil Hall, for the most part well treated on most Savannah plantations. "Not only because it is more agreeable but because pecuniary advantages are always greater." A note in one Savannahian's book of instructions for Thorn Island Plantation cannily emphasizes, "Above all, slaves must be properly cared for and plantation equipment kept in good repair."

Typical was the Hermitage, where slaves were labeled as free hands, three-quarter hands and half hands, who tilled the fields. The plantation was a world unto itself, with cart drivers, carpenters, gardeners, blacksmiths, nurses, cooks for the blacks, and house servants, usually mulattoes, who were noted for their beauty. Working hours were governed by the seasons, with long free afternoons, rest periods in the sultry summers, followed by late-evening work in the cool dusk and free time to till their own gardens and raise poultry for sale.

The system flourished, firmly supported by the planters, the clergy and the press, and its pulsing economic heart was Savannah, where on Factors Walk the price of cotton and rice and slaves was set. Many foreign visitors followed Hall to Savannah, enticed by stories in the northern press, to examine the strange phenomenon of a new feudalism in a free America; but most of them, like the Swedish feminist and writer Fredrika Bremer, agreed that, while slavery was an evil, "under the wise direction of God it will become a blessing to the Negroes. The whites who have enslaved them will make them compensation for their sufferings through the gift of Christianity, and by instructing them in agriculture and the handicraft arts—thus they may be first instructed and then gradually emancipated, and colonized in Africa; the heathen nations of Africa being finally Christianized and civilized through the Christianized and emancipated slaves in America."

Other visitors who had come to investigate the abolitionist attacks against slavery remained to call Savannah the "mother city" of the South and "the garden city where everlasting spring abides and never withering flowers" and "happy Negroes" peddled their wares along the cobblestoned streets. They waxed lyrical over the great houses of a highly cultivated and infinitely charming aristocracy whose hospitality knew no bounds. Savannah was to them the magical center of the cotton kingdom, where on Factors Walk, with its fine skein of wrought-iron bridges, "the Factors handled the fleecy product with so much profit to themselves that the future is now radiant with hope."

It was Savannah that dispatched, in 1819, the first

steamer to cross the Atlantic to Liverpool, where it was lauded in the London newspapers and her Savannah builders were proclaimed the merchant princes of the New World's most promising port. In 1834, the first successful iron steamship in America was riveted together and launched from Savannah; and by 1843, she had become the center of the Central of Georgia Railroad, connected to Macon by 190 miles of rail, the longest track in the world owned by one company. Little recognition was made of the fact that these accomplishments were the handiwork of both slave and free labor.

As for the great plantations themselves, damned by the abolitionist press as bulwarks of evil, they were romantically proclaimed "small kingdoms sufficient unto themselves" by visitors who, approaching the colonial mansions through avenues of live oaks, were welcomed with Madeira, feasted on the seafood gumboes of the low country, enjoyed in the candlelit evenings the flute and piano duets of such couples as the Habershams of Vernon View, and woke to the sweet fragrance of hundreds of orange trees and a luminous sky which defied description.

The factors, the merchantmen, the planters, even the majority of the clergy, agreed wholeheartedly with their mentor, South Carolina Senator John C. Calhoun, that "there never has yet existed a wealthy and civilized society in which one portion of the community did not in point of fact live on the labor of the other."

The slaves themselves seldom rebelled. There were occasional rumors of impending insurrections—one in Savannah which turned out to be a minor fracas ignited by the publication of an abolitionist pamphlet. In adjoining Liberty County, one master was murdered by his slaves, but his cruelty had long been a scandal in that pious Congregationalist community, and sympathy was with the slaves though the law was not. The few missionaries from New England who did come down to preach the evils of the system were brutally and summarily dealt with. Several were lynched. At least one was tarred and feathered, and one, who settled in the state and managed to become a judge, was apprehended in Chatham County and jailed for misconduct for an emancipation decision.

A few planters did have qualms about the system, and manumission was not uncommon in the early days of the nineteenth century. Freed slaves were sometimes shipped to Liberia through the American Colonization Society, but their fate was all too often like that of the thirty-seven blacks freed by a Gwinnett County planter. Thirty died during their first year in Liberia, and the other seven escaped to Philadelphia through the aid of two prominent Georgians who brought them "home again."

By 1859, Georgia was closed to admission of free persons of color, and post-mortem manumissions were prohibited. A planter's last will and testament, was ruled "nul and void." Some clergymen, answering the rising moral condemnation of the abolitionist press, were proclaiming that Negroes were "blackened by some dispensation on high as punishment of the race." But with the clouds of a national cleavage looming ominously, some shrewd observers in Savannah were taking note of the economics of the "great institution" and questioning if it had not actually become an anachronism. Noted one: "Negroes are 25% higher now with cotton at ten and a half cents than they were two or three years ago when it was worth fifteen cents. Men are demented upon the subject. A reverse will surely come."

Clearly, one way to reduce the price of slaves, now averaging $1890 for a hearty male or female on the Savannah market, was to reopen the slave trade, outlawed for fifty years. Savannah planters, having fought this battle for a half century, had given it up. England, France and the United States kept a constant patrol of the African coast, but the dashing, adventurous, ruthlessly unprincipled scion of one of Savannah's oldest families, C. A. L. Lamar, defied the law and brought the last slave ship, the *Wanderer*, to the haunted shores of Jekyll Island in 1859, with such daring that even his sharpest critics still grant him a certain grudging admiration.

Born in Savannah, his middle name, Lafayette, was for the Marquis de Lafayette, French general and hero of the American Revolution, who, as a guest of the city of Savannah in 1825, was present at Charles's christening at Christ Episcopal Church.

Lamar, like most of the hot-blooded and sea-haunted youth of the coastal aristocracy, was fascinated with ships, and as an adventurer, he'd had dealings with Portuguese slave traders when he and his coterie of friends at the Chatham Club heard of the beauty and speed of the *Wanderer*, built in 1856 for a wealthy member of the New York Yacht Club. For Lamar, the *Wanderer* became a passion; he not only determined to possess her, but to use her as a slave ship, and his friends were willing to back him to the fullest.

In that desperate year before the "great institution" was to be finally and irrevocably threatened by "the War," he and a group of friends went to New York, joined the yacht club there, entertained with the inimitable grace and style of Chatham County and managed to purchase the *Wanderer* for, as they vowed over champagne toasts, a pleasure cruise to China. Instead, in the guarded seclusion of Charleston, South

Carolina, the *Wanderer* was outfitted as a slave ship and, in the luxuriant spring of 1859, set sail for the African coast with a crew of staunch rebels headed by Captain John Farnum, a former Indian fighter.

Lamar's past negotiations with the half-caste Portuguese slave traders and the native chiefs stood him in good stead when, after a tortuous journey, the *Wanderer* eluded the patrolling warships, entered the mouth of the Congo River and landed at Brazzaville, where Lamar signed up for delivery of 750 blacks between the ages of thirteen and eighteen, most of whom had been kidnaped in the woods by other Negroes and sold and resold several times before finally being purchased by Lamar and his crew.

His trip back to the *Wanderer* by small boat was intercepted by the arrival of an English warship, which Lamar approached immediately, boarded, introduced himself and his companions as adventurers bound on a pleasure cruise to India, and so entranced the captain with his charm and "refinement" that the British officers accepted an invitation to dine aboard the *Wanderer* the following evening. The ship's store of champagne was brought out. Toasts were drunk and the British laughed uproariously when the roguish Lamar suggested that the *Wanderer* might make a great slave ship. The following day, they embraced in a state of euphoria, the British to pursue an imaginary slave ship which the canny Lamar had hinted was embarking a load of slaves up the coast.

In the wake of the British vessel, the *Wanderer* loaded its cargo at Brazzaville. Eighty men had died en route when the *Wanderer*, paying fifteen thousand dollars for refuge, landed at night on the deserted beach at Jekyll Island. The surviving blacks, packed into the small boats skimming through the marshes, were delivered to the coastal plantations of Georgia, South Carolina, Florida and Mississippi. The steamboat *Augusta* took 170 of the newly captured slaves up the Savannah River and delivered them across the Carolina line to a plantation belonging to another Lamar relative, a senator serving in the legislature then in session in the Georgia state capitol at Milledgeville.

The U. S. District Attorney in Savannah, who had finally gotten wind of the *Wanderer's* landing at Jekyll, swiftly seized the ship and arrested Lamar, Captain Farnum and the few crew members that could be located. Lamar became a subject of heated debate in the Georgia Assembly. A majority of the legislators, to whom Lamar had become something of a hero, felt the federal government had violated the sacred doctrine of states' rights by arresting him. But the New York *Times* lambasted Lamar as the very embodiment of evil.

Lamar, following the hue and cry in the sumptuous quarters that Savannah had provided him as a jail while eighteen townspeople stacked the jury under Judge James M. Wayne, had his cousin L. Q. C. Lamar challenge the New York *Times* editor to a duel. The editor replied with a letter to Lamar, addressed simply "In jail," to which Lamar, in a black rage at the indignity of the address, replied: "I am NOT in jail and the damned Government has not the power to put and keep me there. I am in my own rooms over my office and live like a fighting cock at the *Expense of the Government,* for we notified the Marshal at the beginning that unless he furnished us, we would not stay with him. He submitted our letter to the Judges and they told him to supply us. I can whip the Government any time they make the issue, unless they raised a few additional regiments."

Lamar's trial and his sojourn "in jail" became a veritable

festival for Savannah. While Captain Farnum remained a captive in the city jail, Lamar and three friends stole the keys to his cell and released him, and the two men, with a coterie of sympathetic and ebullient comrades, remained quartered in Lamar's offices on Bay Street while the citizens of Savannah showered them with magnolias, the finest coastal dishes served on paper-thin china, and magnums of French champagne. One of those who elected to share Lamar's merry confinement, Colonel Carey Styles, said after Lamar's inevitable acquittal that the whole ribald episode had been one of the happiest of his life.

Lamar, free again and incorrigible as ever, repurchased the *Wanderer* for four thousand dollars. Savannahians respectfully refused to bid on it. Lamar immediately began to outfit her for a journey to China to smuggle in a load of coolies. While the yacht was anchored off Lamar's cotton compress wharves in Savannah, the newly hired Captain Martin loaded a store of provisions aboard, shanghaied the laborers at gun point and headed for sea in full sail bound for the Congo. He got no farther than the Madeira Islands, where he left the *Wanderer* to row over to a French ship. The crew, in his absence, sailed the *Wanderer* back to Boston and turned her over to the revenue officers there.

But this was 1860. There were some five hundred free blacks in Savannah. The efforts of the African Methodist Episcopal Church to resettle them in Liberia had proved abortive, and it was becoming common to hire Negro artisans, carpenters, brickmasons and boatmen. The planter aristocrats felt their whole way of life was threatened. There was a push to put through the Georgia Assembly a bill forbidding the sale of liquor to Negroes; and a new and tougher law against teaching blacks to read or write was put on the books.

But it was cleverly eluded by such enterprising young slaves as Suzie King Taylor, who studied with thirty-five other slave children, sneaking out of her little home by the kitchen door every morning, her books wrapped in paper "to prevent the police or white persons from seeing them." Later she was tutored by a young white playmate, a student in a convent, and went on to become an aide to the Union's 33rd Regiment, on St. Simons Island.

Clearly the system was breaking up, but only the visionaries could see it. The aristocracy of Savannah still fought the inevitable. "How was a poor man to prosper without a return of the slave trade?" the newspapers asked.

Once again, the *Wanderer* was up for sale. But, by then, Savannah was at war, and despite the bitter prejudice of the Savannah townspeople against doing business with the enemy, Lamar bought back his beloved schooner and dispatched her to Havana, where she brought a high price as a privateer. Captain Farnum became a major in the New York Volunteers and served with such gallantry that he was made a brigadier general. And the *Wanderer*, that swiftest, most beautiful, most romantic and most maligned of schooners, was seized by the U. S. Navy and served out the war as a hospital ship, her virtue finally restored.

Lamar profited handsomely from his venture, promising his outraged followers that the money would go toward the cause of the Confederacy. Inevitably, like Margaret Mitchell's Rhett Butler, Lamar took his stand with the lost cause, and before Sherman reached Savannah, he was killed in the fighting around Columbus, in a battle that was doomed at the outset.

CHAPTER 6

Fort Pulaski

IN THE ROSE-AND-DAMASK drawing rooms of Savannah, talk of "the War" is still likely to prevail. The Civil War was the most dramatic chapter in the city's life, and Savannahians still regard their role in it with patriotic ardor. The fiery eloquence of its orators, the valor of the city's defenders, the nobility and courage of its women have left an indelible mark and given the city much of its romantic sense of history.

Savannah at the outbreak of the war was a bustling city connected with mainline U.S.A. by three railroads, which poured King Cotton into its port. There were two iron foundries, two shipyards, railroad shops, four cotton compresses, a rice mill and several sawmills. By 1860, the population had grown to 13,875 whites and 8,417 slaves and free Negroes. Most of the whites were eloquent exponents of secession. On November 8, following the election of Lincoln and Hamlin, more than three thousand Savannahians assembled in the Masonic Hall, against a background of bonfires, soaring rockets and brass bands, to endorse the resolutions of Francis S. Bartow, who thundered that "the election of Abraham Lincoln and Hannibal Hamlin . . . ought not to be submitted to." According to Savannah historian Alexander A. Lawrence, "A wild shout went up in the hall and echoed back from the throng on the streets. Men yelled until their breath was gone." Said Charles H. Olmstead, who was there, men "hugged each other with passionate embraces . . . in what was probably the most thrilling gathering in my life's experience."

The Savannah meeting triggered the General Assembly of Georgia to appropriate a million dollars for the defense of the state. The prevailing sentiment was voiced by Dr. Richard Arnold, a Savannah physician. "It is a practical question with us, not only as to existence and prosperity, but whether we are to be disenfranchised of our liberties and subjugated to domination of the Black Race." When South Carolina seceded from the Union in January, the General Assembly of Georgia approved an act calling for resistance to the federal government. The action was received with an exuberant celebration in Savannah. The whole town turned out to demonstrate their approval under a large banner in Johnson Square depicting a coiled rattlesnake and the words "Don't tread on me."

On January 2, 1861, three staunch secessionists were elected to the state convention. On the same day, Joseph Emerson Brown, governor of Georgia, made a quiet decision in a Savannah law office to take possession of Fort Pulaski—a difficult decision, as the fort was the property of the United States and Georgia was still in the Union. As Lawrence pointed out, "Viewed in any light, state seizure was an act of hostility against the Federal Government—the most overt step that had been taken by any Southern state up to that time."

FORT PULASKI

Fort Pulaski, which still stands today, as a national monument, one of Savannah's most popular tourist attractions, was the city's main defense against naval attack. Situated on Cockspur Island, between the north and south channels of the Savannah River, it was designed by Napoleon's military engineer and built between 1829 and 1847; it was the *ne plus ultra* of brick and masonry forts. Robert E. Lee's first assignment after graduation from West Point was as an engineer on the fort. As Olmstead describes it, "The Fort is an irregular pentagon surrounded by a broad moat. The gorge faces the west and is covered by an earthwork also protected by a moat. Two faces guard the north channel and two the south —these last having also a bearing on Tybee Island, from whence the attack was to come later. There was one tier of casemates opening on to the parade by large double doors, and platforms had been arranged for another tier of guns on the ramparts. In the casemates were 20 long naval 32-pdrs., mounted on iron carriages, but there was no other armament. Officers quarters, kitchens, storerooms aand magazines are located in the gorge."

One hundred and thirty-four men from three military companies, the Chatham Artillery, Savannah Volunteer Guards and Oglethorpe Light Infantry, set sail for Fort Pulaski to the roaring cheers of an enormous crowd of well-wishers. For Charles Olmstead, their entry into the fort was an unforgettable experience. Years later, he described "the proud step of officers and men, the colors snapping in the strong breeze from the ocean; the bright sunlight of the parade as we emerged from the shadow of the archway; the first glimpse of a gun through an open casemate door; one and all they were photographed on my mind."

The fort at the time was occupied only by an ordnance

sergeant and a caretaker. The victory was short-lived. The first reprisal came in February, when a Union force, secreted in a battery at Venus Point, on the Savannah River, opened fire on the little steamer *Ida* as she was making a trip to Fort Pulaski. The company at Fort Pulaski knew nothing of the battery's existence. It had been erected by a force from Port Royal coming through the Wright and Mud rivers on the Carolina side and was beyond the range of Pulaski's guns. The *Ida* escaped injury, but communication between the fort and the city of Savannah was permanently cut off. The little garrison there, which included four companies of the First Regiment, the Oglethorpe Light Infantry, Washington Volunteers, the Montgomery Guards and the German Volunteers, 385 men under Colonel C. H. Olmstead, were entirely isolated from the mainstream of the war. They knew an attack was imminent, but they had no way of knowing when it would come and how deadly it would be.

They turned their energies to constructing the defensive fortifications that had been laid out by Robert E. Lee, who was then in command of the Military District of South Carolina, Georgia and Florida. Visiting the fort, he had instructed that traverses be built on the ramparts between the guns, ditches dug in the parade to catch shells, the light colonnade in front of the officers' quarters be torn down, and blindages of heavy timber be erected before the casemate doors around the entire inner circuit of the fort and covered by several feet of earth.

Tension mounted during the month of March. According to Olmstead, Pulaski pickets at the water's edge on the south channel reported hearing movements during the night at King's Point, but in the morning light the Sand Ridge was untouched. The only movement was the sweep of sea oats on the dunes. On one occasion, however, three men did appear making "insulting gestures" toward the Pulaski pickets, who fired on them, killing one man with a 32-pounder.

On the morning of April 10, just after reveille, the long vigil was ended. Lieutenant Frank Blair, of the Washington Volunteers, reported to the commanding officer that the summit of the ridge had been leveled overnight. The bushes were cut away and guns were visible, and a boat was spotted approaching Pulaski, waving a flag of truce. Captain F. W. Sims was dispatched to the south wharf to meet the officers who carried the flag and who presented a demand for the surrender of the fort. Sims summarily refused, the officers returned to Tybee and, at precisely a quarter past eight, the first gun was fired.

The Federal guns were situated in eleven batteries stretching along Tybee Island for two and a half miles. Olmstead reported that four of the batteries were at King's Point, armed with 10-inch rifled guns firing Parrott and James projectiles, one 8-inch Columbiad, and four 10-inch mortars. Farther along the line were twelve 13-inch mortars and a few more Columbiads, but the rifled guns and Columbiads at the point inflicted more damage to the fort than all the others combined. When a shot from one of these struck the wall beneath an embrasure and buckled it, the Pulaski forces knew they were doomed.

At dusk, when the commander walked around the edge of the moat, he found the southeast *pan coupé* entirely breached. The parapet above had been shot away and the remnants of an 8-inch gun hung trembling overhead. The two adjoining casemates were badly injured. The moat was filled with masses of broken masonry, and according to Olmstead's report, the dismounted guns lay like logs among the bricks in the casemates.

The enemy themselves did not realize the power of rifled artillery. Reported General Q. A. Gillmore to his government of the Parrott and James guns:

"Had we possessed our present knowledge of their power, previous to the bombardment of Fort Pulaski, the eight weeks of laborious preparation for its reduction could have been curtailed to one week, as heavy mortars and Columbiads would have been omitted from the armament of the batteries as unsuitable for breaching at long range."

The guns from Tybee fired at intervals through the night and in the morning renewed their attack all along the line, while the Confederate fire, its guns decimated, slackened ominously. The breach rapidly widened, and the Federal shells whizzed across the parade, threatening the principal service magazine. It was protected by a large traverse which was believed to be invincible. But at one in the afternoon, it was hit and exploded in the passageway, filling the magazine with smoke and lighting it up with flame.

Wrote Olmstead: "Entirely cut off from any possible chance of reinforcement; the means of replying to the batteries at King's Point reduced almost to nil; and exposed momentarily to the danger of having the entire fort blown up beneath us—the commander felt that the end had come and most reluctantly the order to display the signal of surrender was given."

The firing from Tybee ceased at once, and General Q. A. Gillmore, the engineer officer in charge of the attack, arrived by boat to arrange the terms of surrender. The fort and its armament were given up, and the garrison was made prisoners of war with the exception of the sick and wounded, who were sent to Savannah for treatment. The Fort Pulaski garrison was sent on to Governor's Island, New York, where the officers were confined in Fort Columbus (now Fort Jay), the men in Castle William. The gentlemanly agreement of General Gillmore was tragically violated. Several weeks after the garrison arrived at Governor's Island, the sick and wounded were shipped in, most of them destined to die there, in the final tragic betrayal of the dream of Fort Pulaski, the impregnable fortress of the new Confederacy.

CHAPTER 7

THE War

When Sherman finally arrived at the outskirts of Savannah, after burning Atlanta and cutting a wide swath through Georgia to the sea, the city had but scant defense. Even Sherman overestimated the rebel forces, which consisted of a "mongrel mass" of 9,089 men spread over a front running from the Savannah River to Rose Dhu on the little Ogeechee River—"scarcely more than a skirmish line strengthened at intervals," historian Charles C. Jones described it.

The capture of the little boat *Ida* and of a Central of Georgia Railroad train with the company's president aboard, signaled to Savannah that Sherman was finally "at the gate." By December 11, 1864, after a few skirmishes, the Union forces had closed along the entire Confederate front and were within sight of Savannah. Crossing the Ogeechee Canal, one of the prairie men wrote home that it was a scene of "poetic beauty," punctuated by thousands of voices joining in "Down by the Suwanee River," "Old Kentucky Home" and "Just Before the Battle, Mother. . . ."

On December 13, 1864, Sherman's army sighted Fort McAllister "in plain view, two and a half miles, sullen and silent like a great lion at bay," reported one Colonel Strong, who could see the rebel flag and even the men as they hastily prepared their defenses.

The fort had been isolated from the Confederate world for five days. Major George W. Anderson, commander of the hundred and fifty troops there, many of them "mere boys," having received no response from his messages to headquarters, determined "to defend the fort to the last extremity." He saw only two alternatives, "death or captivity," reports Judge Alex Lawrence in his definitive Civil War history of Savannah, *A Present for Mr. Lincoln.*

Sherman had already sent a message to the Federal Navy of his arrival at Savannah, carried by a scout, Captain William Duncan, in a penciled message concealed in a plug of tobacco. In a perilous two-day voyage to the sea, which carried him right by Fort McAllister, Duncan reached a gunboat in Ossabaw Sound just as his small boat was capsizing. When Port Royal received a dispatch from General Howard that Sherman's "lost army" was entrenched on the coast and ready to take Savannah, "the excitement, the exhilaration, ay the rapture, created by this arrival will never be forgotten by the officers and crews of the Federal vessels who saw the beginning of the end of the war," reported one Federal officer.

Lieutenant George A. Fisher, transported by a tug, steamed up the Little Ogeechee, then transferred to a rowboat to navigate a creek three miles southeast of a rice mill that belonged to a Dr. Cheves, whose adjoining residence at Grove Point had been ransacked, to the delight of his "darkies." Peering through his glass, Fisher spied the Stars and Stripes and, signaling back from the tug, asked, "How can I get to you? What troops are at Fort McAllister?"

"We are now investing Fort McAllister with Hazen's divisions," came the reply.

Soon Sherman, quartered at Cheves' Mill and growing impatient, gave the signal to attack. In the glow of what one officer described as "one of the loveliest sunsets ever looked upon," the Federals, fifteen thousand of them under General William B. Hazen, at three blasts from the bugler, advanced "as with a single impulse."

"Ye Gods! I never saw the like," wrote Strong. "Over the fallen trees that had been slashed for a thousand yards, over snares and pitfalls for tripping up the men, over three rows of abatis and two rows of *chevaux-de-frise*, over the ditch . . . over the huge 13-inch skids made into torpedoes . . . never wavering nor faltering for an instant—with a fierce and impetuous rush to the fort and with a gallantry almost unparalleled and with a wild cheer . . . away they went."

As they scaled the parapets, a dozen flags appeared and the Confederates defended themselves in savage hand-to-hand combat with bayonets and rifle butts, until each one was overpowered, in a desperate battle which lasted only fifteen minutes. "The fort was never surrendered. It was captured by overwhelming numbers," Major Anderson, the Confederate commander, summed up.

That night, Sherman rowed in from Cheves' Mill and dined with Hazen and his prisoner, Major Anderson, at the Pinckney House, near the fort. They were waited on by a servant of the Anderson family, who told the surprised major, "I'se workin' for Mr. Hazen now."

Clawing the air with bony fingers, Sherman told a young

Boston writer a few days later how he had Savannah in his grip but he was going to take his own sweet time in capturing it. Riding on to Howard's headquarters on a Darien Road plantation, he sent instructions to the commanding general of his left wing to place the siege guns "near the heart of Savannah, ready to bombard." Also, he ordered Slocum to send his forces across the Savannah River to block any escape routes from the city.

The week that followed the fall of Fort McAllister was marked by heavy artillery fire and by probing of the defenses to test their strength, reports Lawrence.

Savannah was surrounded, but Sherman was content to wait, wait while the rebels hastily constructed a plank bridge across the Savannah River, wait even when his officers urged him to assault the city of Savannah. Only then did he order preparations for an attack, but he quickly countermanded them, confident that a few days would starve out the Savannah garrison. According to Lawrence, he was jealous of his "reputation for conserving lives."

"Men march to certain death without a murmur if I call on them, because they know I value their lives as much as my own," he once said proudly.

Sherman had lost his blood lust. General Hardee, commander of the Savannah forces, after several unsatisfactory conferences with General Beauregard, in which he warned that "without immediate reinforcement" he would find himself surrounded without any chance of escape, finally wired President Jefferson Davis that "unless assured that force sufficient to keep open my communications can be sent me, I shall be compelled to evacuate Savannah."

On the night of the sixteenth, Beauregard arrived in Savannah to confer with Hardee in the Oglethorpe Barracks.

The two men agreed their first priority was "to complete the pontoon across the Savannah River to Hutchinson Island and thence over Back River connecting with a road to Hardeeville," reports Lawrence.

Hardee's men fell to work with a vengeance, collecting rice flats, ripping up the city wharves for planking, and putting one thousand Negroes to work on the roads. By December 19, the job was done. Hardee had his escape route without any interference from Sherman, a fact that competing generals, Grant especially, never let him forget.

Two days earlier, in a personal note to Hardee, Sherman had demanded an immediate surrender, outlining his strength and warning the beleaguered Confederate general that, if forced to attack, he could hardly control the vengeance of an army "burning to avenge a great national wrong they attach to Savannah and other large cities which have been so prominent in dragging our country into Civil War."

But Confederate communications were still open and Hardee refused to surrender, gambling on an orderly evacuation along the plank road. Sherman's fellow officers were determined to destroy the road, but Sherman remained adamant. He wanted to keep his army together in case of a possible transfer to Virginia, he explained.

On the nineteenth of December, General Beauregard dictated a plan for the evacuation. But let historian Lawrence tell it:

"The field batteries were to withdraw at dark with as little noise as possible and proceed to the city, where they were to cross the pontoon bridge at eight. Ambrose R. Wright's division was to cross at 9 p.m., followed at 11:00 by the division of Lafayette McLaws and, at midnight, by that of Gustavus W. Smith. The garrisons of the various river batteries were to assemble at Fort Jackson, from which transportation was to be provided to Screven's Ferry across the Savannah River."

The next day, an endless stream of wagons loaded with Confederate Army baggage rumbled northward over the pontoon bridge. One of the last soldiers to pass through Savannah recalled the "musical sound, in the dead of night, of the 'clink-clank, clink-clank' of the horses' iron feet as the troopers rode down the brick pavements. When the band struck up 'Dixie,' Union pickets called, 'Played out! Played out!'"

The march was sad and confused that bleak, black night in December. Cornelius Hanleiter recalls the soldiers shouting into the air, "making the night hideous with their oaths and blasphemies while women—'Nympths of the pave,' he called them—roamed the streets" and "horses and men struggled in mud and water along the roadside." A Spalding County soldier wrote what many of his comrades were feeling when he spoke of his desperation "after four years of service . . . to leave my native state to the mercy of a ruthless enemy."

Even the stars were "veiled as if in sympathy," one Savannahian wrote. Late that night, the fires were still blazing as the Confederate navy yard and warships were being destroyed. Only the ironclad CSS *Savannah* was left. She fired on Fort Jackson the only shot that fortification ever sustained. But by seven-thirty the following morning, the *Savannah* was evacuated by her crew and demolished with such a fiery blast that "the explosion rattled windows as far away as Hilton Head," reports Judge Lawrence.

On the whole, Hardee was proud of his evacuation of Savannah. "There is no part of my military life to which I look back with so much satisfaction," he wrote. He had rescued ten thousand of his troops, drastically prolonging the war, felt Secretary of War Stanton.

Mayor Richard Arnold formally surrendered the city to General John Geary early on December 21, requesting "your protection of the lives and private property of the citizens and of our women and children," which Geary was happy to grant.

"Oh Miss! Oh Mizz Lizzie, de Yankees is come, dey is as tick as bees, dey is so many on horses and de horses' tails is standin' out right straight, you just come look out de winder," the little black maid in Elizabeth Basinger's house trumpeted that morning.

It was Barnum's Brigade marching to the City Exchange to raise the Union flag over Savannah. Even as Geary was speaking, a New York *Herald* reporter wrote that mobs of "Irish and Dutch women, Negroes and thevish [sic] soldiers" were looting Savannah's stores. The pillage had been going on all night, the work, said one Confederate soldier, of "the white scum of the city which came out of their dens like nocturnal beasts. . . ." Geary ordered patrols through the streets and, in a few hours, order was restored.

The next day, Sherman arrived at the Pulaski House and wired Lincoln that he was presenting Savannah to him as a Christmas gift, along with "numerous heavy guns, considerable ammunition and about 25,000 bales of cotton."

By nightfall, Sherman had moved into the handsome house of Charles Green, a British subject who insisted the general make it his headquarters and entertained at dinner on Christmas night, answering Sherman's toast with "as happy a little after-dinner speech" as one of the guests had ever heard.

Overnight, Savannah's lovely squares were turned into villages and the streets were hung with the Stars and Stripes, which outraged the women of the Confederacy. But such strict military order prevailed that Major Anderson wrote his wife, "I am rejoiced to hear that G'al. Sherman's policy toward our people is marked with humanity and kindness."

Sentinels were posted everywhere, from the nunnery to the city's many whore houses. "There is the most hoars here that I saw in my life both black and white; I thought Washington had enough but this beats that," wrote one Federal soldier. But for the most part, Sherman's army was entranced with Savannah. It possessed "every mark of wealth, intelligence, refinement and aristocracy," one wrote. An Ohio newspaper correspondent compared it to the "scenery and grandeur and romance of Italy." And Bonaventure Cemetery was to an Illinois soldier "a most grandly solemn and most appropriate resting place for the dead."

As Judge Lawrence points out, Sherman's military dictatorship proved to be benevolent. Savannahians were taken with John W. Geary, military commander of the city, and with the work of the commander, who removed 565 of Sherman's dead horses from the streets, along with 8,311 cartloads of garbage and 7,219 loads of manure, repaired the streets and whitewashed the warehouses along the bay.

But Savannah was a captive city and she never forgot it. "The white people here are the most whipped and subjugated you ever saw," said Sherman. While journalists on the city's two newspapers, the *Republican* and the *Herald*, reported strong Union feeling, a Bostonian reported that "the people look upon the Confederate cause as lost, and therefore come forward and take the oath of allegiance to the United States," and another correspondent said dryly that "the majority of the people would cut all our throats if they could."

Nevertheless, convinced that the war was won and anxious to be done with conflict, Mayor Arnold, responding to a petition signed by seventy-five citizens, called a public meeting and a resolution was passed to submit to the "national authority under the Constitution in accordance with Lincoln's amnesty proclamation."

Sums up Lawrence: "Savannah was at peace with the United States of America."

The Confederate South was outraged. Newspapers as far away as Richmond condemned this act of ultimate surrender, and closer to home, the Augusta *Constitutionalist* labeled the Savannahians "miserable sycophants."

"If there is one lower than any other in the abyss of degradation, the people of Savannah have reached it," wrote their editorialist.

But Savannah's capitulation had an almost immediate reward. Sherman released the Confederate supplies, ordering that rice could be used as a medium of exchange to purchase northern goods. A few days later, a Polish American benefactor, Julian Allen of New York, touched by the city's plight, sailed north to sell the rice and raise money for the beleaguered city.

"It would awaken pity in almost anyone to see the pale, emaciated faces of the women and children," he told crowds in New York and Boston. Three weeks later, the *Rebecca Clyde*, the *Daniel Webster* and the *Greyhound*, sailed into Savannah Harbor, their staterooms filled with dressed turkeys, geese, ducks and chickens.

After getting a venomous lecture from Sherman's chief of commissary when the city fathers requested military labor to unload the vessels—"What lazy, miserable curs slavery made of men," he barked—the mercy ships were unloaded by Savannahians.

"A motley crowd," a New York reporter described the city folk who lined the wharves to receive their free food. "The ragman's fair . . . charity like a kind angel has suddenly stepped in to ward off the wolf which is howling at their doors."

But the rebellious spirit of the black-clad women was unbroken. Many of them refused to leave the house rather than walk under the Stars and Stripes that fluttered over the streets. They shared the feeling of the widow Saussy, who, with five sons in the Confederate Army, prayed nightly that her children would not desert the battlefield to return to Savannah to care for her. To one of them she wrote: "I would rather that each of you had given his life for his country and been buried in an unknown grave than to have such a thing happen with one of my boys."

Those who fraternized with the northern soldiers were sharply criticized, even Chicago-born Nellie Gordon, mother of Juliette Gordon Low, founder of the Girl Scouts of America. While wary enough of the Union soldiers to conceal a small pistol in her belt when she ventured out on the streets, she often entertained old acquaintances of high rank in the Union Army, whom she unabashedly used to find help for her friends.

Even the city's children were far from reconstructed. The Yankees were followed through the streets by urchins chanting:

> "Jeff Davis rides a very fine horse
> And Lincoln rides a mule.
> Jeff Davis is a gentleman
> And Lincoln is a fool!"

The young blacks had another refrain:

"All de rebels gone to hell
Now Par Sherman come."

Still, the women, bereaved and rebellious, had to live. Many of them were accomplished pastry cooks and turned their kitchens into bakeries. "How the mighty have fallen," exulted *Frank Leslie's Illustrated Newspaper.* "If ever God chastened a rebellious people, He has visited our erring brethren." But as Judge Lawrence points out, "Vending cakes was . . . a hardly less respectable calling than that of charging exorbitant rents or interest rates. At least it was more genteel than the occupations of some Savannah females; an old Irish lady, for instance, sold to soldiers whisky described by the 're-publican' as able to 'kill in forty minutes at fifty yards.'"

But these same ladies kept their windows shuttered when the Yankees paraded through the streets "swaying to cadence step, in unison with martial music that filled the air with joy and gladness to the Union cause," followed by a trail of dancing, hopping and clapping blacks, the tail end of a long procession led by General Sherman, "dolled up like a duke."

Even the churches were recalcitrant, refusing to pray for Lincoln, but the black clergymen prayed "heartily" for the President, the government and for Sherman. "Been prayin' for you all a long time, sir, a-prayin' day and night for you, and now, bless God, you is come," a freedman told the general.

Sherman was all but deified at a meeting at the First African Baptist Church, held to inform the blacks of their emancipation. To wild cheers of "Glory, Hallelujah," Chaplain Mansfield French—the White Jesus, the blacks called him—announced, "Your freedom is the gift of God. The President has proclaimed it, and the brave men of General Sherman's army have brought it to you."

Most of Savannah's whites were already disillusioned with slavery. One of them called it "our bane" and said that in peace it had "prevented the development of the ingenuity and energy of the South," and in war had proved a chain around southern necks. But they feared the breakdown of class distinction between blacks and whites and the garrisoning of the city by Negro troops after Sherman left and marched into South Carolina.

Sherman had assured Savannah this would never happen. He was under fire from both sides: the Savannahians, who thought he was too liberal, and the abolitionists, who criticized him as exhibiting "an almost criminal dislike of the Negro." He burned with anger the day Secretary of War Stanton dismissed him from his office on the top floor of the Green house to query Negro leaders about him. But the blacks had only admiration for him. "His conduct and deportment toward us characterize him as a friend and gentleman," they assured Stanton. As for intermingling with whites, they wanted to live to themselves. "There is a prejudice against us in the South that will take years to get over," their spokesman said. The result: Special Field order No. 15, in which the blacks were given the uninhabited offshore islands and the deserted rice fields up to forty miles inward.

Sherman, weary with "Inevitable Sambo," as he called the Negroes, the guarded contempt of Savannah's ladies and the abject terror of the city's children, breathed a profound sigh of relief when he left Savannah to return to the "pine-woods" on January 17 to launch his campaign against South

Carolina. But his officers were reluctant to leave. Wrote one: "Our stay in Savannah has been attended with so much pleasure and good feeling on the part of both soldiers and citizens that we turned our backs on the Forest City with emotions of regret."

They left behind a city decimated by "moral depression." William B. Hodgson, writing in his journal, said that the garrisoning of the city had a "brutifying effect on the people." The men became "excessively distrait," unable to carry on a conversation without repeating themselves two or three times.

"If the present condition of things is to continue, there are no people on the earth who are more entirely enslaved than we will be, and to live here will be impossible to all who have known the blessings of freedom," wrote one Savannahian.

As a final blow to the defeated and demoralized city, a great fire occurred on January 28, consuming over one hundred buildings, including the former Confederate Arsenal. The *Republican* described "the awful grandeur and sublimity" of the spectacle . . . with the flames leaping high in the air, "thrown up in columns by the thirteen-inch shells."

By March, the city was garrisoned by Negro troops and an order was passed deporting the wives and children of Confederate officers across Union lines—an order that had come down from Washington months earlier but that Sherman had refused to execute, evidence of what one Savannahian called "his humanity and good feeling."

The Savannah Volunteer Guards, their ranks decimated by desertion, made a heroic last stand at Sayler's Creek, Virginia, on April 7, 1865. Fighting in hand-to-hand combat which took the lives of thirty men and left twenty-two wounded, the few remaining Volunteers were taken prisoner by the Union forces. Two days later came Appomattox. The war was over.

But it would be almost a century before Savannah recovered. The most daring and courageous of her young men were buried on battlefields across the Southland. Her older men, still in gray, for they had no other clothes, sat around on park benches reliving the war—where had they gone wrong? —and most of the women were garbed in black. The economy was shattered and a way of life was over—a gracious but tragically flawed way, if the diaries and journals of the era are accurate—the best of which Savannah has now recaptured, building on the ashes of the past a renaissance, at last, of the heart.

CHAPTER 8

Savannah Ghosts

AT DUSK, WHEN twilight gilds the rooftops of Savannah and the marshes tremble in the half-light, past and present merge, the supernatural seems natural, reason fails and everything seems possible. This is the witching hour. And in the cream-colored drawing rooms of the city, Savannahians tell ghost stories, recounting them with such soft-voiced plausibility that the weirdest story seems believable.

The city's most famous ghosts reside in the Hampton-Lillibridge House, renovated by Jim Williams, a well-known interior decorator. So offensive were the ghosts of St. Julian Street that Williams had the house exorcised by the Episcopal Bishop of Georgia. When even this failed, Williams gave up and accepted his ghostly guests. Such seers as Dame Sybil Leek, the well-known medium, bustled in from England to hold séances there, and the house was thoroughly investigated by a researcher for the American Psychical Research Foundation.

A typical experience at Jim Williams's house occurred

the night he was awakened at 3:30 A.M. by an intruder's footsteps. The sound, he reported, was like the crush of sand—or was it ground glass?—beneath heavy shoes. Trembling, Williams asked the intruder what he wanted. There was no answer.

The ghostly apparition started toward the door and crashed against an open closet door. Williams hurried to the adjoining library and turned on a light. He could hear heavy footsteps moving around in the darkened bedroom, but he saw nothing there. As the footsteps moved around the room, Williams returned and snapped on a light. Immediately, the footsteps ceased; the mysterious intruder had disappeared.

Ghost hunts became a routine matter for Williams. He was entertaining a friend one night in a downstairs living room when they heard what sounded like a large number of people moving around and talking in low voices on the third floor. The two of them searched all thirteen rooms of the house and found nothing.

While Williams and his visitors grew accustomed to the ghostly apparitions of St. Julian Street, the neighbors continued to be startled by them. Mrs. Lionel Drew, Sr., shuddered at the memory of the night she was awakened by the sound of singing, a rich contralto voice coming from the Williams house across the street. Her husband, also awakened by the singing, joined her in the little room fronting on the Williams house.

"The house was dark on the lower floors, but the top floor, the attic, was brightly lit. I saw dancing figures. The voice I had heard sounded again, and I realized it was a colored woman's voice, a beautiful voice. My husband and I sat together, watching and listening to the party across the street until we both grew sleepy again and went back to bed.

The party was still in full swing at that time. The following day, I saw the man who at that time also lived at the Williams house. I mentioned the party of the night before. He said there had been no party whatsoever. He had just returned from Atlanta that day and Jim Williams was still in London. No one had been at the house at all."

Curious, she later went over to the Williams house. A stairway led to the top floor but the door was tightly closed. She questioned Williams about it, and he replied that the door could not be kept open. Whenever it was left open, someone or something closed it again.

The weird happenings in the St. Julian Street manse can be traced to the time when the house was moved four blocks from its original location on Bryan Street. Even as it was moved, the workmen would throw down their tools and run trembling into the street "after witnessing inexplicable occurrences," reported the Savannah *Morning News*.

Williams himself, with the help of four friends, was investigating the work being done on the interior of the house. They heard what sounded like a crew of workmen upstairs. They went through the house, reported the *Morning News*, searched every shadowy corner, then continued on to the widow's walk, a small platform over the gambrel roof, and heard the identical noises below them. They returned below to find no one there.

Williams did not find his ghosts dangerous until one of his friends, a husky athlete, was almost killed in a spine-tingling event that still brings chills to those who witnessed it. Three of Williams's friends were sitting in the downstairs garden room, an exquisite room that looks out on a terraced garden, when they heard loud voices on the floor above. The athlete went to investigate. Reaching the top floor, he stepped into what seemed to be a pool of cold water. He felt mysteriously drawn to an unfinished chimney shaft which dropped about thirty feet to the basement. He was lying on the floor, shaking and incoherent, when his friends found him. Later, he explained that he felt the only way he could break the force drawing him to the shaft was to throw himself to the floor. It was this event that prompted Williams's decision to have a priest exorcise his newly renovated home. His decision was no doubt hurried when, at the mention of the word "exorcise," a woman's scream punctuated the darkness. When the shriek was heard again, one of Williams's friends rushed from the room only to find a dark-haired man in a white shirt and black bow tie standing at a third-floor window. He thought the man must be Williams, when the owner himself came up the walk wearing a four-in-hand tie, completely unaware of what had happened in his absence.

The rite of exorcism was duly performed by the Bishop of Georgia, but still the ghosts persisted in their weird pranks at the historic house on St. Julian Street. As a final attempt to get rid of them, Williams called in the Savannah Police. A member of the force happened to be in Williams's home when a loud crash sounded in the pipe-organ room, on the fourth floor, the origin of most of the strange happenings. The policeman insisted there was someone upstairs and pursued the sound, a .38 revolver in one hand, a flashlight in the other. When the two men reached the pipe-organ room, Williams saw the door to an adjacent storeroom open, then shut. "He's in that room," said the policeman. But Williams, who always kept that particular room locked, disagreed. Nevertheless, he unlocked the door, and with the policeman, he searched the room, then moved into the attic and out to the widow's walk. "He must have jumped off the roof," concluded the policeman. Williams made no response. The roof was a sixty-foot leap to the street.

His strange and outrageous company of ghosts were put to the final test by Dr. William G. Roll, head of the American Psychical Research Foundation, which conducts research on supernatural phenomena. The former Duke University faculty member spent four nights in Williams's home on a cot in the pipe-organ room.

According to the Savannah *Morning News*, he checked for underground streams and caverns, examined the wiring for magnetic fields and interviewed over thirty-five people who had seen or heard strange things in the house. He concluded that whatever was happening was indeed happening and "was not caused by natural phenomena or human fakery." His theory: The occurrences were caused by some sort of emotional waves, similar to the electronic waves picked up by a television set. The body, so the theory goes, may emit some sort of waves when a person is undergoing a traumatic experience, such as "a suicide, murder or natural death." The waves, in the form of vibrations, are re-created under certain conditions, and these vibrations are the source of the strange occurrences. It is not known what conditions must exist for the vibrations to be released.

The house was bought by Dr. and Mrs. Lawrence Lee, Jr., who have come to cherish its mysterious properties: creaking doors, a woman's scream and clanging chains, and its strange apparitions, most notably an elderly man wearing a gray suit and a white cravat. But they did have one hair-raising experience soon after they moved in. Mrs. Lee relates the story.

"Our 18-year-old son set out some houseplants in a battery jar and placed them on a deep window sill where he sleeps. For extra security, he even roped it in. Just as he had gone to sleep, the battery jar fell on his head. How it didn't kill him, I don't know."

Many of Savannah's showplaces are said to be haunted. The Pirates' House, a favorite restaurant of both visitors and residents, is said today to be the haunt of Captain Flint, the swashbuckling, blood-curdling pirate after whom Long John Silver named his parrot, in Robert Louis Stevenson's novel *Treasure Island*. According to old-timers at the Pirates' House, Flint is still moaning on his deathbed, shouting for rum and damning those who stole his treasure. Herb Traub, proprietor of the restaurant, said the story has been passed on through the years by employees who categorically refuse to climb the narrow wooden staircase to the upper storage room, where an old and trusted employee first claimed he heard mysterious noises—"Old Captain Flint was a-tossin' and turnin' in bed," he declared. Even Traub has never set foot up there by himself.

By and large, Savannah ghosts are a merry lot of revelers, given to late-evening parties or solitary flights of music-making. Take for example the lovely old lady who for years haunted the Owens-Thomas House before it became a historic landmark. Every evening at dusk, she stepped out of the shadows at the garden edge, veiled and remote, wearing a flowing antebellum gown and scented with lemon verbena. She was waiting, it is said, for her horse-drawn carriage. Once, the story goes, she had been the mistress of the stately old showplace. At night she was often heard at the piano, playing poignant, ghostly melodies which were said to be indescribably sweet. When the piano was sold, she left the house, only to return each night at dusk to wait for a carriage that never came.

SAVANNAH GHOSTS

Many of Savannah's renovators find that the stately, crumbling mansions they purchased are inhabited by ghosts. Take for example Mr. and Mrs. James H. Nettles, who own the handsome two-story house at the corner of Victory Drive and East Broad Street. Already in residence there was a ghost whom they nicknamed the Judge.

Their first encounter with the Judge came one night when they were painting in an upstairs room. They heard the front door open and close, then footsteps sounded on the stairs and proceeded down the hall, stopping outside the room. Suddenly, to the Nettleses' surprise, the doorknob turned and the door opened. Apparently there was no one there, but the Nettleses sensed the presence of a powerful but invisible figure. This was their introduction to the Judge. Their maid later met him in an upstairs hall. "He was walking something fierce," she told the Nettleses. After that, she spent her nights in the hall, where she could guard the children from an intruder.

The couple checked to see if a structural defect was causing the strange happenings and unexplained sounds. Windows have been sealed, the foundations firmly enclosed and the house carpeted. But doors still open and close, dishes rattle and lights come on unexpectedly. When they had an elevator installed, it proved to be a boon to the Judge. He no longer walks at night, but the elevator moves about capriciously. "We leave the elevator on one floor and find it on another. It just moves from one floor to another without any reason at all," reports Mrs. Nettles.

Some of Savannah's ghosts have attained a place in the city's history. The houses they haunted have been demolished, but tales of their residence there still persist. For instance, there is the Confederate officer who is reported to have haunted a house on the west side of town one block from Broughton Street. "The man in gray," the homeowners called him. Visitors to the house complained of hearing unexplained noises or seeing "something" moving along the hallways or in the gardens. But the woman who owned the house accepted her ghostly visitor in the Savannah tradition of gracious hospitality, greeting him cordially when she passed him in the hall and often sitting down with him for an afternoon of sewing.

One of the most terrifying encounters with Savannah's ghosts came to a nonbeliever. The house, located near moss-draped Bonaventure Cemetery, no longer stands, but tales of the weird happenings there persist. According to legend, the house was not haunted until a dispute after the death of the rightful owner, when another branch of the family succeeded in establishing its claim and obtaining possession, forcing the original owner's family to vacate the property and die in poverty.

When the original owner returned to wreak his revenge, a nonbeliever in ghosts happened to be sleeping in the library, a large room with portraits of the former owner's family: a man dressed in regimental uniform, a beautiful bride, a woman in stiff brocade and a middle-aged man. The sound of a clock chiming midnight woke the visitor. In the darkness, he heard people milling around behind the curtain of his bed. Rising from the pillow, he saw figures moving through the moonlight. There was a lady in stiff brocade, a younger woman wearing a bridal veil and gown, a middle-aged man holding a roll of parchment and a man in uniform. The military man strode across the room to the middle-aged man and said in a low voice, "Be just, be just. Yield up what is not your own." The figures in the room so closely resembled the

Along the waterfront, near Factors Walk, decaying warehouses are being taken over and remodeled by small shopkeepers and craftsmen of all sorts, creating Savannah's newest marketplace.

The Roman Cathedral of St. John the Baptist, one of Savannah's finest examples of French Gothic architecture.

Interior, St. John the Baptist.

Temple Mickve Israel, 1878. The congregation was founded in 1733, five months after the founding of Savannah.

people in the pictures that the visitor glanced at the portraits on the wall. The frames were empty.

According to a story in the Savannah *Morning News*, "As the middle-aged man shook his head to the gentleman's question, the figures became tremulous and indistinct, then faded into one another."

Years later, workmen digging near the foundations of the old estate found a parchment which established the right of the original owners to the estate. But the wronged heirs were never found.

Most native Savannahians have ghost stories of their own and are happy to relate them to the skeptical. There is, for example, Charles Bennett, whose resident ghost has been seen by his dinner guests but not by him. While they sat at dinner, an apparition "formless but with a form" was seen moving through the hallway.

"Several of my friends have repeatedly seen the same form in different parts of the house," Bennett told a researcher. "One particular friend saw it in the room in which she was sleeping and was frightened enough to leave and sleep downstairs. I later found out that, in that particular room, a past owner, a man, had died of malaria."

Bennett himself has never seen his resident ghost, but he has on several occasions heard sounds of music—"pastorales and pieces of that sort," he recalls. "I learned that one of the previous owners had been a musician. I have found musical items, scores and pieces of scores the man had composed. I doubt that the music comes from any of my close neighbors, as none of them seems to be a fan of that particular kind of music. The music always appears to be coming from the downstairs of the house, but from no particular spot."

Ghost stories have multiplied since the historic renovations became popular. Porter Carswell can tell you about one at East Gwinnett Street at a house now owned by Mr. and Mrs. Norton Melaver. The ghost's image appears in a hall mirror every afternoon at twilight when the setting sun strikes the glass. "Whether it was a man or a woman could not be determined, but it was the image of a human face, and the same form would appear each time," he reported.

Three prominent ghosts reside with the Joseph Solanas at 75 Bluff Drive at Isle of Hope, a house which for over half a century was owned by Miss Mamie Jackson and her two brothers. The Solanas' maid met Miss Mamie in an upstairs room, and later their son met the threesome and reported that they were "making noises like cush-cush." "Cush-cush," the Solanas nicknamed the ghosts. The whole family has now had experiences with them.

Mrs. Lionel Drew, Sr., remembered the ghost at Mrs. Ellen McAlpin's boarding house at the northwest corner of Oglethorpe and Barnard streets. Occasionally she was seen lying down in an upstairs room, and once she and a merry assortment of revelers were heard dancing and singing in the parlor.

Almost every Savannahian has a favorite ghost story. Mrs. Aubrey Waters, can recite dozens of incidents; one ghost even tried to save her life. She was in the hallway one night getting some medicine for her husband, who was ill. "As I hurried down the hall toward the steps, I felt something like a fog trying to stop me or slow me down. In my anxiety, I didn't realize I was so near the steps, and before I knew it, I was tumbling head over heels down the long flight of stairs from the second to the first floor. I'm sure the spirit was trying to warn me."

Mrs. Waters, who is a member of the Association for Research and Enlightenment, founded by Edgar Cayce, believes quite strongly in the spirit world. Sitting at the deathbed of one of her relatives, she saw the spirit literally leave the body, hovering over it like an amorphous blue-and-white flame.

Another Savannahian reports seeing his mother's spirit when she died. He had gotten up to answer the telephone late one night when he saw his mother standing over the crib of her infant son. She wore a blue-and-white gown, and her face no longer reflected the suffering she had endured for months. When he picked up the telephone, it was his sister calling to tell him their mother had just died. She was buried in the same dress she had been seen in the night before, but it was not purchased until the following day.

An East Fifty-seventh Street resident reports seeing the apparition of a small child on several occasions. The apparition of a lady dressed in black and praying with a rosary has been seen in a Liberty Street home, and on Sylvan Terrace, one house has a visitor who materializes frequently; the ghost, it is believed, is the spirit of a deceased neighbor who, when alive, often came over to visit.

In Savannah, the very landscape is haunted. In the surrounding marshlands, the tall grass undulating beneath tremulous skies takes on an unearthly quality. It is said that there a ghostly band of marsh takeys, the little ponies that once roamed wild through the marsh, are rounded up by a wild stallion that comes swimming in from the vast, dark Atlantic. This story is recounted by no less an authority than Miss Bessie Lewis, the well-known historian of Fort King George in Darien.

This is ghost country, and Savannahians have learned to take their ghosts quite seriously as proof positive of the continuity of life. Some of the renovators feel like uneasy tenants in someone else's home, but for the most part, the people of Savannah live amiably with their ghostly company, justly proud of the fact that their city boasts one of the largest and most incorrigible and exuberant collections of ghosts of any city in the nation.

CHAPTER 9

Savannah's Architecture

WHEN OTHER SOUTHERN CITIES were fairly exploding in the sun of post-World War II affluence, Savannah was a sleepy, seedily picturesque little city drifting in the backwaters of the twentieth century. Her hard-driving sons went north to make a living and pen nostalgic valentines to her fading charms; the great houses had deteriorated into crumbling slum dwellings; and drunken derelicts dozed amid the azaleas in the blowsy, neglected little squares laid out by Oglethorpe in 1733. What changed her ebbing fortunes? If there is one single answer, it is Historic Savannah, the nonprofit citizens' group which was born when a sprightly gentlewoman named Anna Hunter rallied her friends to protest the demolition of the old city market for a parking lot in 1954. While Miss Hunter failed to save the marketplace, she did succeed in launching a strong citizens' group, Historic Savannah, to combat the destruction of the city's architectural heritage.

Under the leadership of investment counselor Lee Adler, Historic Savannah went into action so quickly and effectively that, within months, the disgruntled demolitionists were calling it "Hysteric Savannah." From the beginning, they recognized what city planners like Philadelphia's Edmund Bacon had already stated publicly—that Savannah, laid out in 1733, is the "best planned city in the U.S.A." In the era of the bulldozer, the skyscraper and the superhighway, they returned to Oglethorpe's original plan, realizing that Savannah's squares were effective fortresses against the great enemies of the twentieth century: air pollution, high population density, tension and alienation. Around these open areas were some of the finest examples of nineteenth-century architecture in the nation, but they were fast being torn down. Demolitionists were marketing their Hermitage Plantation "Savannah grey" bricks at ten cents apiece to suburban builders. Traffic engineers were eying the squares for through streets; urban developers wanted to clear the "slums" for office buildings; and most of the city fathers regarded downtown Savannah as fit only for business transactions: the good life lay beyond the city limits.

Realizing that restoration was the key to the revitalization of the downtown area, Historic Savannah's first purchase, Davenport House, was restored as a showcase for renovation and a home for the foundation. Known as one of the great Georgian houses of America, it was built in 1820 by master builder Isaiah Davenport and was saved from demolition in 1955. It is renowned for its fine woodwork and plaster work, its Chippendale, Hepplewhite and Sheraton furniture and its superb collection of Davenport china.

Working from a two hundred thousand dollar revolving fund collected over a three-year period, Historic Savannah engaged "the best people in the country" to do an architectural inventory of Savannah. They drew up a four-color map designating some eleven hundred buildings as either exceptional, notable or important, then published a hardbound volume on Savannah's architecture, a work so handsomely illustrated and definitively stated that it was an overnight best-seller in its field.

Although Savannah was razed by fire in 1796, it still boasts a few eighteenth-century houses: notably the Hampton-Lillibridge House, with its handsome gambrel roof and widow's walk, built *ca.* 1797, after the 1796 fire; and the Pink House, also called the James Habersham, Jr., House, built *ca.* 1789, a handsome stucco mansion with quoins and parapets and a stunning Palladian window over the entrance. The interior is noted for its Georgian stair and its strong, simple woodwork.

The Federal Period was marked by delicate fanlike doorways, thin cornices, plaster interiors and elongated columns and pilasters. Notable examples of this era are the Davenport House, built in 1820, the pair of houses on Oglethorpe Avenue, and the superb Independent Presbyterian Church, one of the most important Federal churches in the country.

Savannah architecture came into its own with the introduction of English Regency by William Jay, the young English architect who designed the Richardson-Owens-Thomas House, one of the most beautiful examples of English Regency in America. Now a favorite Savannah showpiece, it was designed by Jay in 1816 for Richard Richardson, a prosperous merchant. It is an outstanding example of romantic classicism, with its columned-entrance portico, winding double stairway, paneled parapet above the main cornice, arches and rare interior design.

Among the other existing houses Jay designed in Savannah are the Scarborough House, and the Telfair House. Jay drew on the orders of both Greece and Rome.

The most recent restoration of Historic Savannah is the Scarborough House, an outstanding example of William Jay's Regency houses, built in 1818 for seventy-five thousand dollars for William Scarborough, who promoted the first transatlantic steamship, the S.S. *Savannah*. It is noted for its portico and its magnificent atrium. This is a richly storied house where generations of Savannahians have gathered in the ballroom banqueting hall. It was deeded to the county for a Negro school, one of the first in the South, but was finally abandoned and purchased by Historic Savannah and designated a National Historic Landmark.

Restoration has been costly. The hastily constructed third story had to be removed and a new roof added to restore the house to its original lines. Structural supports had to be erected and ironwork replaced. DeCourcy McIntosh, who directs the foundation now, estimates the cost of restoration at $615,000, not counting furnishings and replanting of its formal garden. The foundation, having invested $128,000 of its funding, is today fiscally depleted but goes on with a massive fund-raising effort, certain the restoration of the house will serve as a catalyst for restoration of the northwest part of the district, as did Davenport House in the eastern section.

A favorite of tourists is the Juliette Gordon Low birthplace, whose Regency architecture with its historical significance and period furnishings, was recognized as Savannah's first National Landmark in 1965. A living memorial to Juliette Gordon Low, founder of the Girl Scouts of America, it is now owned by the Scouts, who purchased and restored it in the 1950s.

SAVANNAH'S ARCHITECTURE

A striking William Jay Regency building, with its columned portico and ornate statuary, is the Telfair Academy of Arts and Sciences, completed in 1820 for Alexander Telfair, son of Governor Edward Telfair, and bequeathed in 1875 to the Georgia Historical Society as a museum. It is noted for its antique furniture and for its unique interiors, with the original mantelpieces, moldings, cornices and the innovatively shaped rooms for which Jay is so justly famous.

Other architects worked only in the Greek Revival style, seen most dramatically in the Champion-McAlpin-Fowlkes House. It is distinguished by a center hall, a favorite arrangement during the Greek Revival period. The stair is placed in a side hall, and the central hall is penetrated by a circular oculus, or opening. A Temple of the Winds order marks the lovely portico at the front, and the rear piazza is enclosed at both ends, an arrangement that was to become typical of Savannah houses in the following two decades.

About 1855, the Italian villa style and the Gothic Revival were introduced to Savannah. The Green-Meldrim House is one of the outstanding Gothic Revival town houses in America, an invaluable link in the development of the principles of modern architecture which was built about 1840. A cast-iron portico in a delicate Gothic design characterizes the house, and the entrance is asserted by a large pendant. A bay window overlooks the entrance, and smaller oriel windows face the square on the upper floors.

From the beginning, Historic Savannah had to grapple with the skepticism of the financial community, the lack of historic zoning, the pressure of the progressives who wanted to tear down everything, and the plaints of the conservationists who wanted the city preserved as a museum.

Adler argued that Savannah's old houses were big business, that the city needed a first-class downtown neighborhood to support its business district, and that a solid base of talent—and tax revenue—was essential to the city's future. Such formidable allies as the Chamber of Commerce and Forward Savannah were enlisted, and Georgia Tech was engaged to do a study of Savannah's tourist potential. The experts from out of town affirmed that the city's architectural heritage could open the door to a $120-million tourist trade within a four-year period. The Chamber of Commerce, whose conservative policies had contributed to Savannah's reputation as "the best kept secret in America," budgeted eight thousand dollars for a series of newspaper teasers touting everything from Chatham Artillery Punch to the ghostly legends of Button Gwinnett.

Today Adler can look with nostalgic good humor on the days when he was fighting the "Battle of the Savannah Greys" and trying to save some of the city's handsomest mansions a scant thirty minutes before the demolitionist's hammer fell. For Historic Savannah has been an unqualified success. Over 900 of the city's eleven hundred historic houses have been restored; banks are offering 50 per cent loans to restorationists; and Historic Zoning has been voted in.

In addition to the great houses, there are also several miles of row houses restored by such entrepreneurs as Mills B. Lane and Jim Williams, charming nineteenth-century houses of clapboard or "Savannah grey" brick, with deep shutters and elaborate iron grillwork, flanked by walled gardens. You will find them on Habersham Street, East St. Julian Street where stands the haunted eighteenth-century Hampton-Lillibridge House, East Bryan Street, Scudder's Row, Gaston Street, East Gordon Street, East Jones Street, East Charlton Street and East Oglethorpe Avenue, whose many notable restorations include the so-called Lachlan McIntosh House, a stately brick house built in the 1760s as a tavern and believed to be the oldest brick house in Georgia. It is redolent with history, of balls, public meetings and religious services—a meeting spot visited by George Washington in 1791 and the site of early sessions of the Georgia Legislature.

Adler attributes Historic Savannah's success to the fact that the foundation has dealt in real estate, not renovation. Their covenant with buyers requires that buildings be left standing for seventy-five years, that restoration begin no later than six months after purchase, and that, if the house is put up for sale, it be offered to Historic Savannah. "In doing their own restorations, these people have become creatively involved in the life of the city," says Adler.

He is also quick to point out that Savannah has produced a group of restorers ranging from banker Mills B. Lane, Jr., to Mrs. Mary Hillyer, who masterminded the restoration of the ten-acre Trustees' Garden, site of the original garden which the first settlers laid out to grow mulberry trees for silk production, grapes for wine, medicinal and culinary herbs, and other commercially important products.

One of the most articulate of Savannah's restorers is antiquarian and renovator Jim Williams, a militant opponent of "the bulldozer and the architect." He has rescued some twenty-nine houses from both "menaces," including the row houses on St. Julian Street now owned by Mills Lane.

Another noted restorationist is Alida Harper Fowlkes, a gently bred beauty who pioneered the move to town in 1939 when she purchased the stately, columned, nineteenth-century McAlpin House in what was then a crumbling slum area. In those years, she and her mother watched the paddy wagons make nightly rounds of the neighborhood, disguising their own vulnerability to intruders by the simple ruse of placing a man's hat on the entrance-hall table.

Today the Champion-McAlpin-Fowlkes House, its lofty entrance asserted by marble statuary, is a showcase of early-nineteenth-century décor. If Mrs. Fowlkes's good humor ever falters, it is when she speaks of "the second Mrs. McAlpin," the hapless Yankee bride who defaced the mansion's fireplaces with white paint, removed the circular staircase and added a back porch. "I don't like to change things," says Mrs. Fowlkes, who has steadfastly refused to remove the yew trees that veil the columned entrance of her home. Each one was planted to celebrate the birth of a son into the McAlpin clan. "Nobody knows who the sons were," she says crisply, "but the trees are still there."

Acting as her own contractor, Mrs. Fowlkes has managed to restore almost a dozen downtown houses while presiding over two antique shops and making annual buying forays to the British Isles for china and silver, eighteenth-century furniture and fine brass fireplace accessories.

When Mrs. Fowlkes moved into the McAlpin House, no one could have predicted that, by 1968, people like Lee Adler would be concerned that the exodus to downtown Savannah was in danger of becoming "too social, too much the thing to do."

Young couples who five years ago were building split-level homes in suburbia are finding Savannah's old houses perfect for their burgeoning families. The average age of the restorationists is now thirty-eight; most have at least two children.

City life has become an education for them. Says one: "In the suburbs, I'd never have a next-door neighbor who gets up at four every morning to start a fire to warm his house. My neighbor on Pulaski Square does. Our children play together in the park, and we talk. You learn a lot of things in the city—things you don't learn in suburbia."

In the tree-shaded squares, they mingle—flocks of children with their aproned nurses, well-heeled executives, wistful, nodding derelicts, crisp young matrons and idling Negroes with soft Gullah accents. Peanut vendors ply the ancient brick, and at dusk the chimes of St. John's ring out the old hymns: "Just As I Am. . . ."

This is the city, and Savannah's restorers love it. They have managed to close the bars that bordered Pulaski Square, and now they're demanding zoning ordinances, clean streets and better lighting, upgraded schools and better police protection.

The fine points of growth and progress are debated endlessly in Savannah. The skyscraping proportions of the DeSoto Hilton Hotel and the parking lots planned for the new Civic Center were once burning issues. But one thing at least is certain. The push toward progress is not apt to obscure the civilizing properties of the city. "Savannah must be a living city," says Lee Adler, "but Savannah must also remain Savannah."

CHAPTER 10

Pollution and the Water Lords

SEVERAL YEARS AGO, when a former mayor of Savannah dismissed the Savannah River as a "dirty old stream without any hope," he spoke for a majority of Savannah citizens.

Since the day when Oglethorpe came with the first settlers, the river has been the hub of the city's life. Factors Walk on the bluff overlooking the river was the heart of the cotton kingdom, and in the tragic aftermath of the Civil War, the destitute freedmen camped on its banks. As the city revived, the river teemed with ships from all over the world, and its shores were the focus of social life. Recounts one historian: "The populace thronged to the waterfront to view the balconies on River Street which were in their day as much a status symbol as boxes in the horse shoe ring at the Metropolitan Opera."

Five years ago, the mighty Savannah was an aquatic slum that reeked with human pollutant. The river had become an open sewer. Each day, the city dumped the raw sewage of its 135,000 inhabitants into the Savannah River. American

Cyanamid's daily contribution to the river was 690,000 gallons of sulphuric acid. And Union Camp Corporation contributed about 80 per cent of the 100 million gallons of pollutants that were dumped into the river each day.

Ironically, the sites of the great polluters were originally handsome plantations that were the hub of the cotton and rice kingdoms. Union Camp is situated on the site of Hermitage Plantation, where the famed "Savannah grey" bricks were manufactured—bricks still coveted by restorationists. Henry McAlpin bought the Hermitage Plantation in 1818, cultivated the lowland section as rice fields, and converted the higher land for use as a brickyard, a rice mill, a sawmill and an iron foundry, each facing the riverbanks with separate wharves for shipping. Two of the brick kilns were connected by a short railway, the first in the United States. In 1935, the Hermitage was bought by the city of Savannah for ten thousand dollars. Later, Henry Ford bought the buildings and had the mansion taken down and the materials brought to his estate in Bryan County, Georgia, to be used in building his residence, a move hotly protested by the U. S. Secretary of the Interior. In the summer of 1935, the Savannah Port Authority gave the Union Bag and Paper Corporation of the state of New Jersey a ninety-nine-year lease on the Hermitage with an option to purchase.

Brampton Plantation, orginally reserved for the Indians, is today the site of Dixie Asphalt Products. Here once stood the village of New Yamacraw, where Tomo-chi-chi moved his tribe after the English settled Savannah. This was the plantation where Andrew Bryan once preached to the slaves, their first introduction to Christianity and the genesis of the burgeoning First African Baptist Church.

Rae's Hall Plantation, today a huge storage unit, was also

once an Indian settlement, created as a Yamacraw center for trading, stock raising and dairying. In 1830, rice was planted and blooded-stock raising was initiated. By 1911, Rae's Hall was no longer a working plantation. Industry and commerce settled in the area, and railways and wharves were built.

These stately river plantations became the primary sites of the "Water Lords," the major polluters of the Savannah River.

Since Savannah's natives had grown accustomed to the stench of pollution, it remained for Ralph Nader and his investigative team to reveal the raw wound of the river in the lovely façade of Savannah, in their report *The Water Lords*. They found that the roots of Savannah's failure reached into many corners, from legislative weakness to industrial deception, from the technical problems of sewage treatment to the marketing theories of the paper industry, from the biology of the Savannah estuary to the company-town arrangements that had strangled the city for years.

The prime predator in the tragic rape of the river was Union Camp, the largest kraft-paper producer in the world. How was one company allowed to destroy Savannah's greatest resource, her water supply? A combination of factors, chief of which was old-fashioned boosterism, the Chamber of Commerce approach that flourished during the dark days of the Depression. When Union Camp moved into Savannah, both the company and the town were almost bankrupt. Free water, cheap labor and low taxes combined to make Savannah one of the most attractive sites in the nation. In the midst of a severe depression, the city regarded Union Camp as a great boon to the economy. Savannah graciously yielded her innocence to this northern newcomer. It seems never to have occurred to city officials to charge the plant for its use of the water. Progress to Savannah meant new industry, regardless of the fact that it polluted the air and the marshes and with an unquenchable thirst consumed its priceless supply of fresh water.

The water, already polluted by the human and industrial plants of Augusta 160 river miles upstream, took on a coffee-colored brown at Union Camp. The foul waters spread out from the factory in a long brown wedge. As the mill wastes blended in, it spread out over the river. Down through the city it streamed, muddy and foaming, reeking with human excrement as untreated sewage poured into the river through large outfall pipes. The water in front of City Hall often boiled, as pockets of hydrogen sulfide and methane gas rose from the river bed. The river sustained a final blow at American Cyanamid. According to the report of Nader's Raiders, the river water near the plant was often as caustic as concentrated laboratory acid and "has seared the skin of small children who unwittingly dangled their arms in the water."

Savannah made no move to treat its sewage even after the mercury scare of 1970, when the Savannah River from Augusta to Savannah was closed to fishermen because of the contamination of deadly mercury dumped into the river by the Olin Corporation at Augusta. Savannah seemed unconcerned. The lower portions of the river were already off limits to fishermen, closed by an order of the state Water Quality Control Board because of industrial and municipal pollution. And the oyster beds had been closed for over twenty years, condemned because of sewage contamination.

According to the Nader report, the blame for Savannah's pollution fell mainly on one source, the giant Union Camp Corporation. The mill owners spoke their minds with a nineteenth-century public-be-damned eloquence. The director of air and water protection for Union Camp told the Raiders that "it probably won't hurt mankind a whole hell of a lot in the long run if the whooping crane doesn't quite make it." The executive vice-president of the same company, answering a charge that Union Camp dangerously depleted the groundwater supplies, observed, "I had my lawyers in Virginia research that, and they told us that we could suck the state of Virginia out through a hole in the ground and there was nothing anyone could do about it." The company's 1970 annual slogan was "The Name of the Game. Profit Ability." The factory, which was close to bankruptcy when it moved to Savannah, had never spent a dime for pollution control, for the use of Savannah's water, or for its air, which it befouled as powerfully as it did the water.

Ironically, the paper industry is potentially one of the most environmentally safe in the country. Using available technology, it is possible virtually to eliminate the industry's three main offenses against nature: the ever-expanding harvest of forest land, the air and water pollution produced by the mill, and the mound of garbage left over when the paper is thrown away.

The city of Savannah, which was ordered by state officials in 1955 to build a sewage-treatment plant immediately, still had not broken ground for the plant in 1972. Meanwhile, the residual pollution in the marshes and river bed had increased; more and more streams that run through the Savannah estuary network had been closed to swimming and fishing, and the river showed no signs of recovering.

Sewage treatment is not a popular subject or a politically profitable one. During the first two centuries of Savannah's life, the city sent its sewage untreated into the Savannah River. When the city spread south and sewage disposal became unmanageable, sewage pipes were aimed at the raw creeks and streams to the south. During the 1950s, the city did try to meet the problem by installing a few oxidation ponds and a treatment plant for wastes from the suburbs, but the main city sewage, about 16 million gallons daily, still went straight and untreated into the Savannah River, reported the Raiders.

The report of Nader's Raiders received national acclaim. As a reviewer for *The Christian Century* pointed out, the book "has national rather than merely local impact . . . for it mirrors what has happened all over the United States." Initially a study of the pollution of the Savannah River, the Raiders' investigation of city files and county tax records revealed a "cesspool of corporate thinking, and public administrative and legislative misfeasances. . . . The same political and economic arrangements that ruined the river impede its cleaning and also fill the air with obnoxious and dangerous contaminants. Industries profit and homeowners pay in a tax system which shortchanges the county government several million dollars yearly."

Probably the most dangerous practice of Union Camp was unlimited use of ground water, which dangerously lowered the water level and artesian pressure of the aquifer, the rock stratum of porous limestone which soaks up water in highland Georgia and South Carolina and dips farther and farther beneath the surface as it moves through eastern Georgia.

"Maps that indicate major drops in the water level show a core of depression at the Union Camp wells," reported *The Christian Century*. As industrial pumpers continued their steady suction from those areas that showed already depressed water levels, the direction of the flow of water—which used to move out to sea—was reversed, and water from all directions flowed toward the pumping point. The enormous pull exerted by Savannah drew salt water into wells less than fifty miles away, and some hydrologists predicted that, within a decade, rural residents of the coastal plain might as well be stranded in Nevada.

The city seemed finally to have found a solution. For the next twenty years, Savannah's water users would be paying a 24½ per cent "pollution abatement surcharge" on their water and sewer bills. Savannahians complained that the surcharge was either too high or too low.

But today the picture has been dramatically changed. Sparked by the national outrage over the Nader report, Savannah went to work on its scandalous pollution record. A 6-million-dollar sewage-treatment facility has been completed by the city, and Union Camp, which had come to symbolize the struggle between environmentalists and industry, has become something of a hero in the fight against air and water pollution. It has completed a 39-million-dollar network of air-pollution controls and has constructed a 4-million-dollar clarifier at the plant. On Hutchinson Island, it has constructed a giant, 200-acre, 17-million-dollar aeration lagoon to treat 33 million gallons of waste water per day. It is a masterful feat of engineering, with an earthwork dike system that resembles the great pyramids, and an under-the-river pipeline capable of carrying more than 60 million gallons of waste to the offshore lagoon—offshore because the land necessary for the lagoon was simply not available, and had to be dredged up from the river.

Savannah's waters show the result. When fishing enthusiasts like Lee Adler can boast, discreetly of course, about catching a 200-pound marlin off Savannah's shores, it's proof positive that the fish are back. So are the tourists. Clean waters pay dividends and not all aesthetic.

CHAPTER 11

Resorts

SAVANNAH'S OCEAN VIEW is shockingly limited. Tiny Tybee Island is marred by a chain of bawdy honky-tonks and echoing, decrepit, unpainted old houses, relics of a brighter era. The torn and ravaged beach marked by Tybee Light and the ruins of Fort Screven, today is a conservationist showcase for erosion. Affluent Savannahians frequent other spas: the Savannah Inn and Country Club on Wilmington Island, the gracious accommodations on Hilton Head Island or the more recently developed Fripp Island.

Known familiarly as "the Old Oglethorpe," the Savannah Inn was once the musty, rococo, vaguely sinister lair of the Teamsters hierarchy, a sad, seedy palace of a hotel which had fallen into such disrepute and disrepair that "no one went there any more." But it was magnificently situated on the Wilmington River, and the pleasure boats that cruise the Intracoastal Waterway often paused there for cocktail parties at the dock. It boasted one of the finest golf courses in the

Southeast, and its banquet and meeting facilities were among the largest on the Georgia coast.

It remained for the giant Hotel Corporation of America, HCA, to move in with a $4-million-dollar investment, the services of a superb decorator (James Frew, of Miami), a crack golf architect (William Byrd, of Atlanta) and a management team with a flair for image building. The result: the Savannah Inn and Country Club, with 115 guest rooms, two villas and four cottages, is today one of the poshest resorts in Georgia.

With genius and no little daring, Frew has combined Colonial décor with Mediterranean design, expanded the guest rooms by one third, and added a shopping arcade of charming boutiques patterned after Savannah's historic Factors Walk. With a sumptuous ballroom that accommodates a thousand people, the chandeliered Emerald Room for dining and dancing, a sunny yellow-and-white card room, paneled meeting rooms, and a neat George III bar furnished with antique chairs from the Bank of England, the hotel itself is stunningly elegant.

The 72-par, 18-hole golf course, originally designed by Don Ross in 1927 and modernized by William Byrd at a cost of $1 million, is studded with four artificial lakes and shaded by moss-hung live oaks. Green fees are modest, golf clubs are available, and the 19th hole is a plush and paneled clubroom dominated by an open hearth.

Close by are the tennis courts, stables, and a marina that can accommodate five 50-foot yachts and offers underwater repair, a bar, and restaurant services. There is an olympic-size pool and facilities for fishing, water skiing, scuba diving and sailing.

An added attraction is the Peter Tondee Tavern, named

Private residence at Bull and 36th Streets.

After the Civil War, Victorian houses laced with white-painted gingerbread took their places among the Regency and Greek Revival antebellum houses on Savannah's squares. Above, left, a detail from the ornamentation of the house on the preceding page. Right, detail from an unrestored house, showing elaborate wrought-iron braces.

This house on East Liberty Street combines Queen Anne simplicity with Victorian decoration.

Above, left, the Hamilton-Turner House, 1872, on Lafayette Square, is a particularly fine example of Victorian architecture. Right, twin houses on East Jones Street, built in 1883, the story goes, for two sisters.

Built in 1882, this house, at 19 West Gordon Street, is typical of Savannah's tiered and shadowy verandas and its brick-and-wrought-iron-walled gardens.

Restored row houses. Above, 406–12 East Liberty Street, built in 1882. Right, McDonough Row on East Charlton Street.

Columbia Square. A fountain splashes in the sun, overlooked by historic Davenport House, of Georgian design, and by the massive Victorian house on the left, now a place of business.

Art Nouveau door, unrestored house.

Savannah architects have made much use of wrought or cast iron, illustrated in all the remaining photographs. Above, the back porch and garden of the Green-Meldrim House.

for Savannah's revolutionary-era tavern keeper. It is decorated in the eighteenth-century idiom with deep wood tones, copperware, red plaid carpets, enormous old rum kegs, and an unforgettable view of the Wilmington River through panoramic windows. The hard-bound wine list is excellent, there is a wide selection of continental beers, and the menu includes Lobster Savannah and Chateaubriand at prices that are not unreasonable.

The queen of resorts is Hilton Head Island, just across the state border, in South Carolina. Hilton Head is not so much a resort as it is a way of life. Its population includes the highest concentration of Who's Who listees gathered anywhere in the United States. On the island, they have found Nirvana. There are no neon lights, no billboards, no tall buildings, no traffic. The sordid commerce of Savannah Beach seems light-years away. The timbered houses merge naturally into the towering oaks and palmettos; and life centers around the Plantation Club, where the talk is largely of golf scores and water hazards and days are measured to the pleasant pace of golfing, tennis and boating, horseback rides, hiking and bird watching. Wild life is discreetly curbed into arboretums, nature trails and forest preserves. And if the shattering impact of the coastal wilderness is lost, there are compensations. The sentineled gates also shield the islanders from the harsh facts of hunger on neighboring Daufuskie Island, where 125 welfare recipients live out their lives in mute desolation, a lingering and tragic aftermath of the Civil War.

Hilton Head owes its imaginative development to the vision of three men: Fred and Orion Hack, of Port Royal Plantation, and Charles Fraser, pioneer of Sea Pines Plantation, South Beach and Harbour Town. In their battle to protect the integrity of Hilton Head, they have staved off BASF, a giant German chemical plant, and a Russian natural-gas manufacturer whose dredging operations threatened to severely lower water tables and destroy the shrimp and oyster fishing.

The continued battle to preserve the island's ecology goes largely unnoticed by vacationers and residents of Hilton Head. There is just too much to do. Take for instance the life at Sea Pines Plantation, forged out of a wooded turkey farm by developer Charles Fraser who has created probably the best-known spa in modern resort time. Here the indefatigable birdwatchers of the Audubon Society have identified 260 species of birds.

There is horseback riding at Laston Field Stables, and leisure strolling from the winding paths of the Sea Pines Forest Preserve to the wide expanse of unspoiled beach. There is hunting from the Honey Horn Shooting Preserve, skeet shooting, yachting and sailing in Calibogue Sound, fishing by charter boats—the red snapper banks are thirty-five to forty miles out, and seventy miles out is big-game fishing in the Gulf Stream. Sea Pines Plantation has three championship 18-hole golf courses—the Ocean Course, the Sea Marsh Course, and the Harbour Town Course. The Harbour Town Course, site of the Heritage Golf Classics, is the newest and has been cited by *Sports Illustrated* as being "just about the best new course that anyone has built in ages."

There is tennis on twelve championship tennis courts in the plantation, four all-weather courts at the Plantation Club, and eight rubico quick-drying courts at Harbour Town. And there is a Young Peoples Recreation Program for 2-year-olds up to 17-year-olds, which offers everything from shell hunting to exploring hikes through the plantation.

A newcomer to the Island is the Hyatt Resort Hotel, which opened in February 1976 at Palmetto Dunes, a resort community of posh houses built on a network of waterways. It boasts 372 rooms and suites, a 17-court Racquet Club, two 18-hole golf courses presided over by Bob Toski, world famous teaching pro, a 25-meter swimming pool, a health club and sauna, excellent restaurants, unique cocktail lounges, an exciting nightclub and an arcade of fashionable shops.

The success of Hilton Head triggered another venture off the coast, at Fripp Island. When a Savannah banker heard Jack Kilgore's request for a $250,000 loan to finance a bridge to the little-known Island, he barked incredulously, "A quarter of a million dollars to build a bridge to nowhere?"

The last link in a chain of marsh-studded islands off the coast of Beaufort, South Carolina, Fripp was then only a tangled palmetto jungle ringed by virgin beaches. It had been uninhabited since the seventeenth century, when English privateer John Fripp used it as an outpost to prey on Spanish vessels; although he is said to have buried his gold somewhere in its moss-hung thickets, no treasure hunter has ever bothered to search for it. Forbidding and inaccessible, the island remained the well-kept secret of the lyrical-tongued Gullahs who raked its shores for oysters and a few sports fishermen who cast for cobia in the inlet they call "Skull."

Not until 1960 was Fripp rediscovered, this time by Jack Kilgore, a soft-spoken Columbia, South Carolina, trucking salesman who, trolling for marlin out of Beaufort, happened upon Fripp's deserted beach and in a moment of what his detractors were to call pure madness, resolved to buy the island. The "Bali Ha'i" instinct is deep-rooted and compelling, but Kilgore, a salesman with a wife, three children, and an outsized mortgage, had every reason to resist it. He envisioned the island as a resort community of fine houses and excellent recreation facilities, all designed to preserve intact Fripp's natural beauty and splendid isolation. When he returned to Columbia to look for backing in the project, most of his friends told him quite frankly that he had gone off the deep end. But with the success of nearby Hilton Head already assured, Kilgore finally managed to drum up the six hundred thousand dollars purchase price of the island, the first step in the pioneering venture he called a "pure gamble."

While he struggled to finance a bridge to Fripp, Kilgore subdivided the island, barged in a bulldozer from Hunting Island, shuttled prospective property owners into Fripp by motorboat, laid pipes to pump in water from nearby St. Helena, engaged golf architect George Cobb to transform the palmetto-thicketed northern end of the island into an 18-hole championship course, and settled on the Polynesian architectural theme which reflects, perhaps unconsciously, his innate romanticism about Fripp.

In the mid-sixties, to the beat of a calypso band and the ring of rum-punch toasts, Kilgore finally introduced Fripp to an awe-struck assemblage of influentials from the world at large. The center of the weekend gala was the million-dollar Lai Tai Inn, a Polynesian retreat with contemporary lounges and meeting rooms, pool side terraces, and gilt-and-glass restaurant. The five-course meals include such coastal delicacies as she-crab soup and broiled Spanish shrimp with Tyrolean pancakes and French pastries. The inn's sixty units, stunningly done in Spanish contemporary with muted green and gold accents, overlook one of the most beautiful beaches on the Atlantic. The Polynesian theme is sustained from the towering wooden tikis that guard the entrance to the pink swizzle sticks in the Outrigger Lounge.

No one strolling the four-mile beach at Fripp, watching its spectacular sunsets, savoring its enormous silence and its lingering sense of history, could fail to understand the peculiar enchantment that seduced Kilgore into his grand gamble. Stark-white heron swoop over the fields of marsh grass; sea turtles still paddle up to the dunes, and deer flit through the palmettos at dusk.

At the same time, the most pragmatic of businessmen could not fail to realize the practical wisdom of Kilgore's gamble. Fripp, by way of Augusta on Highway 278, is less than six hours from Atlanta, forty-five minutes from Savannah, and a short, 17-mile detour off heavily trafficked Highway 17, which links Virginia with Florida's east coast. With an average mean temperature of 65 degrees F., it is ideally suited for year-round recreation. Its very size—three thousand acres—gives it an island atmosphere that is unique: the Atlantic is seldom out of sight.

With an eye to the island's year-round tourist potential, Fripp Island Resort, Incorporated, has invested heavily in golf. The 18-hole, 72-par championship course is, according to the editors of *Golf Digest*, George Cobb's finest to date. A retired navy captain, one of the first to play the 6,538-yard course, is said to have complained: "This is a grand golf course. Too bad they didn't build it on land." With some twenty lagoons, Fripp probably has more water hazards than any other course in the country. Cobb himself regards it as "possibly the most picturesque course I ever built." The 9th hole plays 380 yards, with lagoons to the left and the right; from the cup, you can see the ocean, and a brisk wind threatens the best of shots. An 18-foot alligator guards the lagoon to the right of the green at the 384-yard, par-4 13th hole, and the 15th, a par-3, is hazarded by a 160-yard lagoon. The Atlantic itself hazards the 18th, which plays 380 yards along the ocean to a green fronted by another lagoon and backed by the sea. Green fees are waived for guests at the Inn; electric carts are available; and the 19th hole, just off the pro shop, is a sunny, informal bar overlooking a dazzling stretch of ocean.

Coastal Carolina is basking happily in the glow of Fripp's success. In Beaufort, a historic little town of gleaming church spires, columned Colonial mansions, and walled courtyards, the Daughters of the Confederacy, who ten years ago were pushing for a monument to the Civil War dead, are now conducting house and garden tours for a growing band of tourists, and moonlight boat tours of Savannah visitors are arriving nightly.

CHAPTER 12

Savannah and Conrad Aiken

SAVANNAH HAUNTS ITS lovers like a beautiful, infinitely mysterious woman. And no matter how far they stray, how many affairs they have with other climes and other cultures, they invariably return, if not in fact, in fantasy, to "the garden city."

Of no one was this more true than of Conrad Aiken, who left Savannah as a boy of eleven, after a shattering tragedy, to divide his residence between Massachusetts and England. He roamed Italy, England, and Spain, producing perhaps the most significant body of work—poetry, novels, criticisms—of the twentieth century, to return to Savannah after sixty years, when the crowning achievement of his lifetime, the third-person autobiography *Ushant*, was republished, and to help spark a cultural renaissance destined to establish Savannah as one of the most cultivated cities in the United States. He had by then won almost every literary award that can be accorded a man of letters: the Pulitzer Prize for Poetry, the National Book Award, the Bollingen Prize, the gold medal for poetry of the American Academy of Arts and

Letters. He occupied the chair of poetry at the Library of Congress in 1950–52, having been made a fellow in American letters in 1947 and a member of the American Academy of Arts and Letters in 1956; but his final accolade and the one he cherished most, though such literary peers as T. S. Eliot would have twitted him for it, was that of Poet Laureate of Georgia.

A native of Savannah, born August 5, 1889, he was the eldest of three sons and a daughter of a Harvard-educated physician, Dr. William Ford Aiken, and his cousin, the former Anna Aiken Potter, whose New Bedford father was William James Potter, a Unitarian minister, widely renowned for his lectures against religious dogma and for his espousal of Darwinism, a towering figure whose sermons led his congregation "into the wilderness of unbelief." His influence was deeply ingrained in the family. Aiken called him the "guiding light" who illumined the cosmic thought that gave a third dimension to his incandescent, symphonic lyricism.

But the Unitarian faith was considered heathen by his Negro Catholic nurse Selena, and when Aiken was an infant and ill with fever, she was so fearful about the welfare of his immortal soul that she stole him from his crib and delivered him to the Cathedral of St. John the Baptist to be baptized in the Catholic faith. Years later, when she died, she was clutching a picture of the four Aiken children, blurred with her kisses.

Aiken's childhood in Savannah was freewheeling. While his mother was busy with her younger brood, he roamed the waterfront, sea-haunted, entranced by the ships, the cargoes from exotic ports, the ancient Gullah work songs of the longshoremen, the gulls mewing with ineffable sadness or, on luminous days, soaring with rapture. In *Ushant*, he describes his impressions of those days: "his inescapable mother, the sea"; "the moss-streamed live oaks beside the Thunderbolt river"; the tall shuttered windows of his three-storied house with its brick stoop and iron railing and brownstone steps; the sheltering oaks; the blood-red glitter of cassina berries in winter; "the sense of the infinite, the limitless cruelty of light"; "the sequined shadows of the peach and chinaberry tree"; the rich dirt of the Savannah streets; "the latticed doors to the fetid alley" where he ventured out "to take inevitable possession of his own private world."

At the age of nine, already gripped by an overpowering sense of destiny, he wrote his first poem: "The lions that waited all the day, / Lie concealed in the grass for their prey," it began, a moral poem that captured the essential irony of life in the fact that the lions caught the antelope and the men shot the lions.

And then, abruptly, it all ended. He felt the first ominous threat to his carefree life when his mother, putting him to bed one night, pledged him "to protect her." Not long after this, he was wakened by an early-morning quarrel in his parents' bedroom, then a stifled scream, and then the sound of his father's voice counting "three" and two loud pistol shots.

He tiptoed into the dark room, where the two bodies lay motionless and apart and, "finding them dead, found himself possessed of them forever," he wrote in *Ushant*.

In his autobiography, he recalls the rows of chairs in the drawing room in Savannah, the two somber coffins parallel before them. The Unitarian relatives came down from New Bedford, and he vividly remembers walking down the stoop for the last time, "the funeral wreaths and purple ribbons" on the door behind him, a copy of *Jackanapes* in his hand and the epigraph from *Tom Brown's School Days* in his head:

"For I'm the poet of White Horse Vale, Sir, with Liberal notions under my cap."

Aiken lived first with a great-aunt in New Bedford and then with his uncle William Tillingghast's family in Cambridge, from about 1903 on. At Middlesex School in Concord, he edited the school paper and then went on to Harvard, where he came to know John Reed, Walter Lippmann, E. E. Cummings, Robert Benchley and T. S. Eliot, who became his closest friend. The two men were to share their writing experiences, to converse and laugh together throughout their lives.

Aiken was elected class poet at Harvard, but he never served in that office. He was put on probation for cutting classes to turn a Gautier short story into a poem and, full of righteous indignation, resigned from the university in protest, only to return a year later and graduate in June of 1912.

It was at Harvard that Aiken discovered Freud, when the Viennese psychiatrist delivered his famous Clark lectures in America. So powerful was the grip of Freudian psychology on the death-haunted young poet that it profoundly influenced his first novel, the semiautobiographical *Blue Voyage* (Scribner's, 1927), and six years later, *Great Circle*, with its fusion of musical structure and psychoanalysis, a novel so powerful and original that literary friends, among them the poet H.D., brought it to the attention of Freud, who called it a masterpiece and invited the young writer to Vienna as a subject for free psychoanalysis. But Aiken refused, fearing, as he explained later in a moving short story, that the cure of his neurosis might mean the death of his creativity. Years later he was to regret his decision, but that was only after his work was done and he had published in *Ushant* an exploration of the human psyche that often surpassed the limitations of

Freud and has been called by such critics as Mark Schorer the major literary achievement of the twentieth century.

Aiken was an authentic man of letters who, after a few teaching stints at Harvard, supported almost completely by his literary efforts himself, his first wife and three children, his second wife and finally his Lorelei "of the spirit," artist Mary Augusta Hoover, his wife of 36 years. His paying jobs included editorial work for *Dial*, four years as British correspondent for *The New Yorker* (he wrote the "Letter from London" and the "Report on Tennis"), and reviewing books for magazines in the United States and England. But he was first and foremost a writer, who authored four novels, forty short stories and many volumes of poetry.

Music I heard with you was more than Music is one of the great love lyrics of all time, and *Morning Song of Senlin* has become a classic. His early works—*The Charnel Rose, The House of Dust, The Jig of Forslin* and *Pilgrimage of Festus*—reveal the evolution of the poet, the passion, the romantic lyricism, the musical cadence and Freudian psychology that led to the long sequence of symphonies *The Divine Pilgrim*, published in 1949, which won him his first recognition as a major poet of the twentieth century. But it was the publication of his *Selected Poems* (1929) that won him a Pulitzer Prize and introduced him into the serious anthologies, making him familiar to every school child who ever took a literature course. Of his short stories, done for the pure love of the form, "Silent Snow, Secret Snow," the stream of consciousness of a young boy relapsing into isolation and a death wish, is most often anthologized. Still, there is much to be rediscovered in Aiken's great outpouring of literature. His masterpiece, *Ushant*, begun when he was consultant to the Library of Congress and republished when he retired to Savannah, was so far ahead of its time, so profound, so novel an art form, that the critics are just beginning to catch up with the poet's vision, his lyrical, compelling exploration of the outer reaches of the spirit of man.

During the major part of his literary life, he lived in Massachusetts or in England, avoiding the competition and the literary rivalries between his contemporaries, avoiding even the spotlight and refusing to be lionized, enjoying in country drawing rooms and English pubs the literary luminaries of that golden era of poetry—Ezra Pound before madness seized him, and almost always T. S. Eliot. He was endearing, charming, renowned for his gaiety and wit, though weighty books have been written about his chaotic, death-haunted subconscious, his dreams and his unresolved Oedipus complex.

Yes, Aiken was a lover, courageous and committed, refusing to take refuge in madness, though he once struggled with the demon suicide. Still, he refused to ally himself with any literary school or even find a haven in the sanctuary of dogmas as Eliot embraced the Episcopal Church.

"The thing," he wrote in *Ushant*, was not to retreat, never to retreat, never to avoid the full weight of awareness and all that it brought, and above all, never to seek refuge from it in the comforting placebos of religious or mystical dogma. The pressure would become, for some, too great to bear. The temptations too, would be insidious. The security in conformity, in joining and belonging, was to prove too seductive for a better man than D (Aiken's pseudonym), including the best of all, the Tsetse (Eliot's).

His lifelong journey toward literary excellence, toward love—and he loved the company of women—and toward self-discovery led him first to England and on to Europe, for, as

Schorer points out, Europe for Aiken "was a perpetual promise, a vision of unimaginable discovery"; yet all through his life, "it is instructing him in the vision of the west; of America"; and in the end draws him back to the west and to himself. Inevitably, Aiken returned to Savannah to a row house at 230 East Oglethorpe Avenue next door to his boyhood home, a tall, shuttered house with a high stoop and an iron railing, overlooking Colonial Cemetery with its towering oaks and azaleas and the ancient blurred tombstones of Savannah's revolutionary heroes and duelists. Conrad Aiken had come home, at first to spend his winters and then to live; to spark the lagging Poetry Society by judging manuscripts for a prized award set up in his honor by Mrs. Craig Barrow of Wormsloe, that attracted manuscripts from all over the country; to instigate art shows, one by his much-acclaimed wife, Mary Hoover. But more important to write—a children's book, poetry, and limericks and to annotate the crowning achievement of his literary lifetime, Ushant, which Mark Schorer recognized as a "profoundly original document . . . an almost stunning outpouring of prose, an incredibly subtle reconstruction of the soul's landscape, a work of the most extraordinary sinuous, subjective affirmations: I became, I am, simply, magnificently that."

He told Atlanta *Journal* writer Andrew Sparks that "in a way I never stopped writing about Savannah—it is not always identified as Savannah, but there it is. You couldn't grow up in a place like this without being fixed on it forever. I think it's one of the prettiest cities I've ever seen and will always be if they'll keep on keeping filling stations and loan companies off the corners." For all the tragedy he had suffered, Sparks found him a gay and humorous personality. Recuperating from a heart attack, he was scribbling limericks for amusement, reading them aloud in a rich, lyrical voice and exchanging them with Eliot, who was recuperating from an illness in England. He gave one to Sparks as a memento:

> "Thaid a thad little man from Duluth,
> I've got a thore tooth and it'th loothe.
> What I need ith a martini
> With oh juth a teeny
> Or even not any vermouth."

Savannah adored him: a shaggy, balding man with a redhead's complexion and a taste for colorful attire—purple or orange ties, blue cotton shirts, herringbone tweeds—a shy man initially until warmed to rare wit and laughter by good talk, mostly of the literary world, of Faulkner, Pound and always Eliot, who genially acknowledged him, to Stephen Spender, to be the better writer.

Despite his waning energies, he was lavish with the young, with Malcolm Lowry, whom he regarded almost as a son, and with the fledgling poets of Savannah, whom he encouraged through the Poetry Society of Georgia with his advice and friendship.

And there were always the many Savannahians—journalists, writers, poets, artists, doctors, musicians, teachers and *aficionados*—who gathered in the comfortable quarters on East Oglethorpe Avenue in the second-floor drawing room to indulge in conversations that glittered like the frosted beads on his silver martini goblets.

Shortly before his death, in August 1973, Savannah honored him with a Conrad Aiken Day, preceded by a special symphony concert and celebrated in the newspapers with a potpourri of old photographs of the poet and his family, tributes from the city fathers and one of his dramatic poems, *The Coming Forth by Day of Osiris Jones,* with its recollections of what he always called the "magically beautiful city."

> "Magnolia trees with white-hot torch of bird
> The yellow river between banks of mud
> The tall striped lighthouse like a barber's pole
> Snake in the bog and locust in the hole."

CHAPTER 13

Skidaway Island

THE TWENTIETH CENTURY has come at last to Skidaway Island. For centuries, the little twelve-mile island slumbered off the coast of Savannah at the juncture of the Wilmington and Skidaway rivers. Its golden marshes, undulating with the tides, gave it a haunting, unearthly quality, and its moss-shrouded oak forests were like great cathedrals. But at long last and inevitably, the bulldozer and the developers have arrived. The intruders are the Branigar Corporation, a subsidiary of Union Camp; the Skidaway Institute of Oceanography, a research institute under the aegis of the state Board of Regents; and a state park now open to the public.

While there are purists who would resent any interloper on Skidaway Island, indications at this point are that the island is being developed with vision and sensitivity.

The island's past development is rich in history. After the Indians, came the settlers who, under the leadership of General Oglethorpe, arrived on the *James*, the second shipload of Englishmen to settle in Georgia. They included six single men and five with families. There were a wigmaker, a clogmaker, a ropemaker, a weaver, a dyer, a tavern keeper, a bookbinder and a soldier, but no farmers, no one equipped to forge a livelihood out of Skidaway's stubborn soil.

Their first days on the island were marred by threats of Indian invasion. The settlers constructed a guardhouse on the northern tip of Skidaway to house them until they built dwellings of their own. Life was harsh. The forest was intractable, the soil sandy, the climate either too hot or too cool. The settlers soon joined the Savannah Malcontents; only blacks, they believed, could till the soil of Skidaway. They thirsted for rum, which they believed could alleviate their suffering, and like the others, they objected violently to the "tail-male" system of inheritance.

When Thomas Causton, the Savannah storekeeper, visited Skidaway, he reported that the people were "generally idle." He did report that Thomas Mouse, the clogmaker, had improved his land. Mouse was to become a symbol of beleaguered industry. After his neighbors gave up and moved to Savannah or Charleston, he kept doggedly at his post on Skidaway, trying to till the land, while he reported that he could not even afford shoes for his children. He finally died of overwork, leaving just one settler, William Ewen, who, after years of privation, abandoned the island.

In 1752, the Trustees relinquished their charter and Georgia became a royal province. Sea Island cotton was introduced in Georgia in 1767 on Skidaway, and the island entered a new era under the leadership of John Milledge, an entrepreneur who was a member of the first Commons House of Assembly. His son, John the younger, became one of the "Savannah Liberty Boys" at the age of eighteen, raided the royal powder magazine in Savannah in 1775, sent the spoils to the Continental Army in Massachusetts, and arrested Chief Justice Stokes and the royal governor, James Wright. He participated in the successful attack on Savannah by Georgia patriots and the French forces under Count d'Estaing. At the age of twenty-three, he was appointed to the office of Attorney General of Georgia.

John Milledge established a residence on the new island plantation, which became known as Modena, a name probably taken from the province of Modena in Italy, famous for its silk culture. Milledge returned to politics and served in the state legislature before he was elected governor of Georgia in 1802, and later served as a United States senator, becoming the first president pro tempore of the Senate.

Modena became a flourishing plantation, producing corn, cotton, mulberry trees and oranges, while maintaining sheep, cattle, hogs and horses. Milledge owned some thirty-two slaves, valued at twelve thousand dollars. After his death, his son tried to carry on, but the plantation had to be auctioned off, for $2,375, in the 1840s. The island was ravaged during the Civil War. Union troops landed on Tybee without resistance, successfully laid siege to Fort Pulaski and plundered the nearby island. The plantation buildings on Skidaway were burned and the lands laid waste.

In 1877, Stephen B. Bond purchased Modena Plantation and revived cotton culture, cattle raising and timber. Modena has had other owners, many of them prominent Savannahians, among them John H. Estill, head of the Savannah *Morning News*; Rufus E. Lester, mayor of Savannah; Ralph Isham, a wealthy gentleman adventurer decorated for valor during World War I; and during the 1930s, the Robert Roeblings of New Jersey, who still live on the island.

Lovely Mrs. Roebling is the matriarch of Skidaway. Her

scrapbooks are filled with memorabilia of life on her island, where she and her husband raised five children. When they arrived on Skidaway, the island was much like it had been when the English landed there. While they cleared the land and built their house, they lived on their schooner, the *Black Douglas,* which was anchored off the northern tip of the island.

The family was almost entirely self-sustaining. They raised pedigreed Angus cattle and maintained a three-acre vegetable garden. Teachers were brought over from the Isle of Hope to teach the Roebling children. Their childhood on Skidaway must have been magical. The young Roeblings had a Confederate battery to explore, and three shell rings, which yielded an inexhaustible supply of Indian artifacts, among them a burial urn that contained the remains of a child. The derivation of the rings is still not known, but many historians think they grew up out of the Indians' feasts of oyster roasts, while others think they were used in Indian religious rites. With World War II, an era passed for the Roeblings. The *Black Douglas* was commandeered for training service and, after that, was sold to the Department of the Interior.

Recently, the development of thirty-five hundred acres of the island was launched by the Branigar Organization, Inc. Branigar's plans call for a posh resort patterned after Sea Pines Plantation on Hilton Head Island. The prestigious firm of Sasaki, Dawson, Demry Associates has been hired, as the developers put it, "to produce the ultimate compromise between people, amenities and nature preservation." It was Sasaki who spearheaded the development of Hilton Head. Arnold Palmer was brought in to help design the golf course, which he describes as "a truly honest golf course."

Union Camp, still sensitive to the charges of Nader's

Raiders, which made it the villain in its study of Savannah's air and water pollution, *The Water Lords,* has taken enormous steps forward to insure that it will not despoil the fragile beauty of the marsh-bound island. Dr. Herb Windom, of the Skidaway Institute of Oceanography, has taken on the post of consultant and is now engaged in research experiments to convert the river spoil, by dredging, into a new marsh. He also advises on matters such as estuarine balance, use of fertilizer on the 18-hole golf course and green-belt areas, and soil-erosion prevention.

"I became involved with the Branigar people because they have demonstrated a very real concern with taking proper care of the environment," he says.

The care taken to preserve Skidaway intact is personified by Harold Beck, project manager of development for Branigar. Beck has catalogued every tree on the island, and with an unerring eye, he presides over the clearing for golf-course and home sites. He points proudly to the fact that, in 1973, Union Camp spent $53 million for pollution control.

Skidaway State Park has proved to be one of the most popular parks in Georgia. It was visited by almost thirty-eight thousand people the first two weeks it was open, tourists and campers who found among its gnarled, veiled oaks, the surrounding marshes and lovely estuaries an oasis much as it was when Thomas Mouse first tried to eke out a living there. It boasts excellent facilities for campers, a swimming pool and bathhouse, and day-use picnic areas. As Parks and Historic Sites Director Henry Struble says, "It's a park that fills a void that has been very prevalent for many, many years."

Perhaps the most interesting development on Skidaway is the Oceanographic Institute, where research on oyster culture is today the overriding concern. Open to the public, the institute offers daily lectures on the ecology of the marshes, with water tours of the surrounding marshes. Its educational program augments that of the prestigious Savannah Science Center and caters to students of all ages.

Although the bridges that link Skidaway to Savannah have robbed it of its remote, insular quality—it is only minutes away from downtown Savannah—it has, after two centuries of neglect, finally come into its own.

CHAPTER 14

Dining and Drinking in Savannah

"Certainly every school boy knows that famous remark made by the late Mark Hanna: 'I care not who makes our Presidents as long as I can eat in Savannah,'" wrote Ogden Nash in his introduction to the *Savannah Cookbook*, "a collection of old fashioned receipts from colonial kitchens."

With its distinctive coastal cuisine, its legendary hospitality, pungent libations, and high-hearted appreciation of the exquisite camaraderie of the table, Savannah has a tradition of fine dining and civilized drinking that dates back to the birth of the colony of Georgia and flourishes today at a dozen outstanding restaurants, in the dank and picturesque little bistros along the waterfront, and in all the better kitchens, where housewives swear by Harriett Ross Colquitt's old *Savannah Cookbook*, whose first "receipt," Mrs. Habersham's Terrapin Stew, calls for three large terrapin, boiled and picked, one pint sweet cream and a half pint of sherry.

For two centuries, Savannah's cuisine was a secret, not by intent but because the Negro cooks who presided over the kitchen were artists who could never communicate the ingredients and procedures of their culinary masterpieces.

> "Cookin' lak religion is
> Some elected an' some ain't
> An' rules don' no mo mek a cook
> Den sermons make a saint," as Mrs. Colquitts'

cook used to say.

In the old days, Savannah housekeepers bought either from the city market—it was its demolition that sparked the birth of Historic Savannah by Anna Hunter—but more often from Negro vendors who plied the streets, carrying on their heads great baskets of shrimp, crabs and oysters, and filling the morning air with lyrical Geechee cries of "Crab by 'er! Yeh swimps! Hey oshta!"

Dinner traditionally was at 2:00 P.M., followed occasionally by madeira "tastings"—and no one ate "out," though the taverns since Peter Tondee's day have usually been filled.

Today, one of Savannah's most distinguished restaurants, The Olde Pink House, buys its seafood from the fishermen at Thunderbolt and from a couple, teachers both of them, who fish in the afternoon and deliver their catch directly to owner Herschel McCallar, Jr. Listed by many epicureans as one of the twelve outstanding restaurants in the country, The Olde Pink House is the culinary center of Savannah's renaissance.

The Olde Pink House was well qualified to become Savannah's most outstanding restaurant. Built *ca.* 1789 by James Habersham, Jr., a revolutionary hero who helped finance Savannah's role in the war, it was constructed on the site of an original land grant from the Crown of England to William Grover in 1759 and is known as the oldest 18th-century brick mansion in Georgia, one of the few houses to sur-

The Mercer-Wilder House on Bull Street.

The window lintels of these two houses appear made of plaster; they are instead wrought iron. Left, 19 West Gordon Street. Right, the Noble-Hardee House, Bull and Gordon Streets, on Monterey Square.

Wrought-iron-and-brick gateway, private home.

The Armstrong Mansion, built in 1917, at Bull and Gaston Streets.

Wrought-iron detail, the Savannah Volunteer Guards Armory, on Madison Square. On each side of the building are two of these devices; they are the bolts for shafts running completely through the building and meant to keep it from buckling in the event of an earthquake.

Gas lamp near the waterfront. Wrought-iron balcony, Scudder's Range.

Cast-iron pelican newell post at the entrance to the John LeBey House, Bull and Taylor Streets.

Gate to a private garden. The grapes are done in gold leaf over iron.

vive the fire that razed Savannah in 1796. In 1802, after Habersham's death, it was purchased by the United States as a branch of the U. S. Bank. It became the Planters Bank of the State of Georgia in 1812, the first incorporated bank in the state, and was used by Sherman's aide, General York, as headquarters during the Union occupation of Savannah in the waning months of the Civil War.

When Herschel McCallar, Jr., a native of Savannah, who had presided over the famed Gaslight Restaurant in a Sacramento suburb, purchased the "Pink House" with Jeffrey Keith in 1970, it had fallen into neglect and disrepair and, abandoned after its varied history, was threatened by the demolitionist's hammer. The two men appreciated its architectural distinction, the quoins, the end parapets, the stunning Palladian window over the entrance, its magnificent Georgian staircase and its strong, simple woodwork. Its location was superb, only a block from the river, overlooking Reynolds Square, which is dominated by a statue of John Wesley, founder of Methodism, and treasured as one of the most beautifully planned squares in the city.

McCallar spent months researching and restoring the house, calling on Savannah artist Anne Osteen to reproduce its original color, a Jamaican pink tinged with orange, accrued through the years as the original soft red brick bled through the patina of white paint. Mrs. Osteen recaptured the color so authentically that it is today a notable addition to the Martin Senour palette of historic colors. The original interior, modified by the tenants of two centuries, was also restored to the splendor of Habersham's time.

At lunch, amid drawing rooms graced with fine mantled fireplaces and historic portraits, among them one of James

Habersham, Sr., himself, Savannahians and a growing host of visitors enjoy the extraordinary cuisine of the low country—riverfront gumbo, shrimp creole, crab au gratin, batter-fried shrimp and crab cakes—served with Savannah Bar-b-que Beans, yellow rice cooked in chicken stock, The Olde Pink House's famed yeast puff rolls laced with a touch of bourbon, and crowned by "Anne's black bottom pie" or the House's Trifle (homemade cake layered with custard, flavored with sherry and heaped with whipped cream), all served by waitresses in period gowns.

At dinner, The Olde Pink House, hosted by French Canadian Monsieur Frank La Fremiere, takes on a Continental aura. Guests toast the Manse's historic elegance with Planter's Punch, a traditional and potent nectar of dark and light rum, fruit juices, grenadine, pineapple juice and banana liqueur peculiar to the coast. The old house echoes with the conviviality of a high-hearted evening of *haute cuisine*—Grenadine of Beef (two small filets mignon char-broiled and served with a wine mushroom sauce), Chateaubriand, Spring Chicken Plantation (broiled chicken glazed with an orange sauce and herbs on a bed of yellow rice), Chicken *Cordon-Bleu*, Broiled Baby Flounder stuffed with crabmeat dressing, Royal Beef *Bourguignonne*, and the seasonal surprise, listed on the parchment menu as "Mr. and Mrs. Habersham's dinner," a provocative invitation to re-enter the eighteenth century and savour what the Habershams had for dinner that evening two centuries ago.

Downstairs, The Olde Pink House is another world, a tavern warmed by two roaring fireplaces flanked with deep leather couches and paneled with the weathered boards of a dismantled slave cabin, hung with seascapes and decorated with ship models. Here such simpler dishes as shrimp salad are served on plank tables, and the revelry continues until 2:30 A.M. weekdays, midnight on Saturdays.

Today, the exotic tongues of a dozen foreign countries mingle with soft low-country accents in the drawing rooms of the "Pink House" as thousands of visitors join the native *aficionados* to rediscover Savannah's oldest, most renowned and exquisite achievement: the art of gracious hospitality, in which fine wines and extraordinary cuisine, the ambience of a great and storied home, cultivated hosts and considerate service make dining out one of the rarest pleasures of the human heart.

Even more colorful than The Olde Pink House is the Pirates' House, a mid-nineteenth-century seamen's inn, now a labyrinthian restaurant, lounge, gift shop, museum and art gallery situated in the historic Trustees Garden, Savannah's first major restoration, done under the dynamic leadership of Mrs. Hansell Hillyer, wife of the then president of the Savannah Gas Company. The garden was originally the site of America's first agricultural experimental garden. When the experiments inevitably failed, with Oglethorpe's high hopes perishing in the sandy soil of Savannah, the garden was divided into building lots. The Pirates' House is a modest frame structure with blue shutters (to keep the haunts away). Often, during rum bouts, while notorious river pirates mingled with sailors from all over the world, drugged and drunken seamen were dragged off and shanghaied onto waiting vessels, waking to find themselves on the high seas bound for some exotic port. One Savannah policeman stopped by the Pirates' House for a friendly drink and awoke on a four-masted schooner bound for China. It took him two years to make his way back to Savannah.

Savannah legend has it that this is the Pirates' House

memorialized by Robert Louis Stevenson in *Treasure Island*, where Captain Flint, who originally buried his gold on Treasure Island, died in an upstairs room, calling for more rum, and his ghost still haunts the attic.

Herb Traub, who acquired the restaurant when it was being used as a museum, has expanded the Pirates' House to twenty-three rooms, where he nightly serves at least six hundred guests. But for all the restaurant's dazzling success, Traub has retained its romantic flavor with rough-hewn beams and candlelight and eighteenth-century memorabilia: old fish nets and rusty anchors and, on the patio, a wishing well with an oaken bucket two centuries old. The walls in some rooms are hung with original local art; new exhibits are constantly being mounted.

The menu boasts the widest and most varied selection of low-country dishes to be found on the coast. Favorites are oysters Savannah, creole shrimp, Miss Edna's seafood bisque, and Mrs. Traub's crab casserole. Generously, Traub shares his culinary secrets with the public in the *Pirates' House Cookbook*, which has become a culinary Bible for Savannahians and tourists alike. It is a novel cookbook, studded, amid its wealth of coastal "receipts," as Savannahians call them, with recipes for such things as Happiness Cake, which calls for one cup of good thoughts, one cup of kind deeds, one cup of consideration for others, two cups of sacrifice, two cups of well-beaten faults and three cups of forgiveness.

Savannah abounds in good restaurants. Two favorite luncheon spas are the Exchange, down on the waterfront, now a tradition among the local businessmen who gather there for sandwiches and beer at lunch; and Mrs. Wilkes' Boarding House, which boasts Georgia's best country cooking

—hot biscuits, fresh vegetables, fried chicken, meats and seafood.

At night, there is the Boar's Head, set high on the cobblestoned waterfront, its entrance dramatically lighted by *flambeaux*. It has lost none of its original flavor. Guests dine by candlelight on prime ribs, the specialty of the house, with a rare view of the harbor and the ceaseless activity of the great ships along the waterfront.

More and more popular is Tassey's Pier at Thunderbolt, the terminal of many a harbor tour, an admittedly modern restaurant with a fine seafood menu and a circular bar where one can watch the shrimp boats steaming in with their day's catch. Other notable restaurants are Rex Epicurean, noted for its delicate squid stuffed with shrimp and its Greek pastries and Carey Hilliard's, with its superb hush puppies.

For all its fine restaurants, the most authentic Savannah cuisine is still to be found in the city's great houses. A favorite is the simplest: hominy. Mrs. Colquitt makes it this way:

BOILED HOMINY

> It's grist before it is cooked and hominy afterwards. . . . So wash your grist in several waters, cover it in the proportion of one part grist to three parts of water and put it on the stove in a double boiler with salt to taste. Let it boil for one hour or more, stirring frequently to keep from being lumpy.

Game is a favorite in the low country, especially venison steak. Here's how Mrs. Colquitt cooks it:

It should be fried with very little lard, or butter, turning frequently. They should be treated as a child and never be left alone a moment . . . and when they are fried to a turn, they should be covered and allowed to simmer slowly until tender. The backstrap is the best to use for steaks. Slice with the grain of the meat, pieces of about one-inch thick. Broil in butter with pepper and salt to taste. Just before taking off, add sherry wine to flavor.

But shrimp gumbo is by far the most popular of Mrs. Colquitt's coastal dishes. Her recipe:

SHRIMP GUMBO

2 quarts boiled shrimp	1 large tablespoon butter
½ cup vinegar	3 onions
6 large tomatoes	A little salt
2 bay leaves	1 quart okra
1 tablespoon Worcestershire Sauce	Parsley-thyme
	1 red pepper
Several bird's eye peppers	Salt, pepper, pinch sugar

Boil shrimp with two onions, one cup of vinegar and a little salt in two quarts of water. Take out when done and save water for gumbo stock. Make a roux of the other onion, the butter and the flour, previously browned, and cook smooth with the hot shrimp stock. Add the okra (previously cooked), the shrimp and the seasoning, and let simmer a short time before serving.

Today, Savannahians dine late, after cocktails, for Savannah is a hard-drinking town and renowned for its beverages, most particularly Chatham Artillery Punch, the potent creation of the famous Chatham Artillery, the city's oldest military organization. This renowned libation is a "suave and deceitful brew," as Mrs. Colquitt points out, which only Savannahians know how to handle with poise. The recipe:

CHATHAM ARTILLERY PUNCH

1½ gallons Catawba
½ gallon St. Croix rum
1 quart Gordon gin
1 quart Hennessey brandy
½ pint Benedictine
1½ quarts rye whiskey
1½ gallons strong tea
2½ pounds brown sugar
Juice 1½ dozen oranges
Juice 1½ dozen lemons
1 bottle maraschino cherries

Make stock with above from 36 to 48 hours before time for using. Add one case of champagne when ready to serve.

Chatham Artillery Punch has been served to most of Savannah's visiting dignitaries (among them, according to tradition, President James Monroe), who have come away dazed and raving about its unique properties. But it is simply not exportable. At a memorable gathering in Atlanta, it was introduced so explosively that the party, held at an eminently respectable address, was raided by police, who found the city's outstanding journalist perched atop a piano singing "Dixie."

Other libations dear to the hearts of Savannahians are Bacardi rum punch, mint juleps, scuppernong wine and Planter's Punch. These are served mostly at home.

On the waterfront, where Savannah's night life is centered, the more conventional beverages are served in the little ballast-lined bistros. Here the cosmopolitan flavor of the city is most pronounced, with sailors from a hundred ports mingling with the tourists and natives at the crescent-shaped bars.

Evenings are apt to be long and carefree, for Savannahians love a party and are loath to leave one. This is a city that prizes good food and good drink as basic to the good life, and it takes its pleasures seriously. An evening in Savannah, starting with the waterfront bistros, going on for a late dinner and winding up for a liqueur at the bar of the DeSoto to listen to the blues played on a plaintive guitar is the formula for a magnificent evening, one that will not soon be forgotten.

CHAPTER 15

Sightseeing in Savannah

On St. Patrick's Day, after the great parade when the fountains are flowing green in Johnson Square and the tall, minted gin drinks take on an emerald hue, the revelers at the Pirates' House lift their glasses to Savannah in the same spirit of lyrical ardor with which their forebears once toasted Dublin.

Like Dublin, like Paris and San Francisco, Savannah is not so much a city as a region of the heart, a quality of grace and leisure which has almost vanished from urban life. Few American cities inspire the loyalties that Savannah engenders in both visitors and her native sons. Her admirers have ranged from General Oglethorpe, who conceived her, to General Sherman, who ravished her; from the generation of Negro blues singers who mythologized her, to the hard-headed financiers who cherished her through the bitter years of a prolonged depression. Somehow they preserved her ageless beauty and her unique life style. And today, when the cities that once obscured her are fighting for their lives, her admirers are gallantly ushering her into her finest hour as a prototype of the urban environment.

Her squares, laid out by Oglethorpe in 1733, make her unique among American cities. They are the city's principal drawing card for environmentalists, journalists, city planners, architects and a growing number of tourists who come to visit and remain to stay, many of them for a lifetime.

Lured to the city by a spate of national magazine articles, many of them began their love affair with Savannah at the Visitor's Bureau in the lobby of the DeSoto Hotel, where some of the city's loveliest and most gracious matrons hand out brochures outlining walking tours, bicycle tours and rental tapes for auto tours that comment on the colorful history of the squares.

Johnson Square, earliest of the twenty-four original squares, was laid out in 1733 and was named for Oglethorpe's friend and helper, Governor Robert Johnson, of South Carolina. *Sojourn in Savannah*, the invaluable little guide book by Betty Rauers, Terry Victor and Franklin Traub, describes it as a crossroads in history. The early colonists met there to gossip, draw water at the well just south of the square, post public notices and tell the time of day from the sun dial, which was replaced in 1933 by the Society of Colonial Wars in Georgia. In 1825, French General Marquis de Lafayette laid the cornerstone for the historic monument that marks the grave of Revolutionary War hero General Nathanael Greene. Savannahians gathered there in 1847 for a public reception for Daniel Webster and his wife. When South Carolina seceded from the Union, the whole town met at Johnson Square, whooping the rebel yell, to unfurl from the Greene monument the secession flag.

Wright Square, named for Sir James Wright, last of the

royal governors of Georgia, was laid out in 1733. Here a massive granite boulder from Atlanta's Stone Mountain commemorates the burial in 1739 of Tomo-chi-chi, the mico, or chief, of the Yamacraw Indians. It was Tomo-chi-chi who befriended Oglethorpe, presented him the site on which Savannah now stands, and who, with his nephew, made a historic trip to England to visit King George. A monument to William Washington Gordon, founder and president of the Central of Georgia Railroad, dominates the square.

Greene Square, laid out in 1799 and named for General Nathanael Greene, is circled by house markers that record the original colonial street names of revolutionary days: King Street, after the monarch of England, now President Street; State Street, formerly Prince Street, after the Prince of Wales; and Congress Street, formerly Duke Street, after the Duke of York.

There is Columbia Square, patriotically named for the new republic, which is flanked by Davenport House, headquarters of the Historic Savannah Foundation.

Lafayette Square was laid out in 1837 and later named for the Marquis de Lafayette after his visit to Savannah in 1825; and Pulaski Square, in the center of one of Savannah's largest redevelopment areas, is circled by handsome new restorations of former slum dwellings that once housed as many as twelve families. Monterey Square was laid out in 1847 and named as a tribute to the capture of Monterey, Mexico, by General Zachary Taylor's American forces. Dominating its towering red azaleas is a monument to General Casimir Pulaski, the young Polish nobleman who died a hero's death in the American Revolution.

Madison Square, laid out in 1839 and named for President James Madison, features a monument to Sergeant

William Jasper, hero of the Siege of Savannah in 1779, a granite marker pointing out the southern lines of British defense, and cannon commemorating Georgia's first two highways. Chippewa Square, honoring American valor in the Canadian battle of Chippewa, is dominated by the city's most notable statue, a handsome bronze figure of James Edward Oglethorpe, designed by Daniel Chester French, dean of American sculptors. The colony's founder faces south toward his enemy, the Spanish, whom he defeated in 1742 at the Battle of Bloody Marsh, on St. Simons Island.

Washington Square, recently landscaped and today one of Savannah's most beautiful squares, was laid out in 1790 and named for President George Washington. It was early surrounded by small houses "of great architectural merit," affirms *Sojourn in Savannah,* which deteriorated into reeking slums, and has now been stunningly restored on a street of oyster shells and serves as a model of the rejuvenation of Old Savannah.

Queen of Savannah's many parks is Forsyth Park, dominated by a magnificent white fountain erected in 1858. Here stands a lofty sandstone monument to the Confederacy designed by Robert Reid, of Montreal, in 1874. It is flanked by busts of two Confederate heroes, General Lafayette McLaws and Brigadier General Francis C. Bartow, within an iron-railed enclosure, and here, too, are the Marine Corps marker; the fragrant and unique Garden for the Blind, a project of Savannah Garden Clubs; the Spanish-American War Memorial, and craft- and workshops for Savannah's senior citizens.

Savannah's unique aura of romance, of history and adventure, derives from the waterfront, where coughing tugs, lumbering freighters, and sleek new liners bring to the city a sense of teeming foreign ports, of vast, mysterious seas, of distant lands and unknown peoples. This is Savannah's link to the past. It was here that Oglethorpe landed. The site of his damask-lined field tent is marked by a marble bench on Yamacraw Bluff, and it is here that Savannah maintains its burgeoning shipping industry.

Dominating the bluff is Factors Walk, a flank of red brick buildings named for the antebellum cotton brokers who there conducted the commerce that made cotton king and who were the hard overseers of the romantic myth that was the Old South. With its ramps paved with cobblestones brought as ballast in early sailing ships, the district is redolent of Savannah's past as queen city of the cotton kingdom, that rich, golden, deeply marred era of columned plantations and storied leisure, a legendary Eden shored up by a slave system that still gives Savannah, for all its ineffable beauty, its intrigue, its mystery and romance, a strangely sinister aura of ancient evil.

Here are the Washington guns, two bronze cannon captured from Cornwallis at Yorktown, a bread-and-butter gift from the general to the city that entertained him so royally in May 1791. Here, too, is the former Cotton Exchange, completed in 1887, with its exquisite iron work railing, the city exchange bell built in 1799, and a Revolutionary cannon.

In the shadow of Factors Walk, the cobblestoned waterfront is lined with some of the most charming and original boutiques, arts-and-crafts shops and wine-and-cheese shops in the country. Many of them were built by one-time tourists to make their lives there.

Here also are dank little bars and bistros, walled with ballast stones or old brick, lyrical with the aching sadness of Negro blues and jazz, tinkling pianos and the accents of a dozen foreign countries. Here is the Military Museum, with its outstanding collection of Confederate weapons, cannon and yellowed documents—stunning memorabilia of the War Between the States. Here, too, is the Ships of the Sea Museum, Mills B. Lane's treasure of nautical artifacts: a colorful and romantic collection of ship models from every era of sailing, a ship's carpenter shop, and ship's library, a ship's chancery and an export exhibit.

The most romantic figure on the waterfront is a bronze statue of Florence Martus, "The Waving Girl," who, between 1887 and 1931, became an international figure by waving a white cloth by day and a lantern by night to the ships that passed her brother's lighthouse on Cockspur Island. Nearby is the Harbor Light, erected in 1852 to warn mariners of the peril of underwater vessels scuttled by the British in 1779. Here, too, are two of Savannah's most notable restaurants, the Boar's Head, site of Confederate headquarters during the War Between the States, and the Exchange, which has become a tradition among Savannahians, who crowd its ballast-flanked dining rooms at noon every day for drinks and sandwiches. Overlooking them is Emmet Park, a tribute to Robert Emmet (1778–1803), Irish patriot and orator, a sweeping, oak-shaded vista, a splashing fountain of "Savannah grey" brick, commemorating the city's three most famous ships, the steamship *Savannah*, the U.S.S. *Savannah* and the nuclear ship *Savannah*.

The very heart of Old Savannah is the Trustees' Garden and Village. Here, in 1733, the colony's Trustees launched an ambitious agricultural experiment, sowing plants and herbs from all over the world, which were to make England the leading exporter of silk and wine. The mulberry trees and the grape arbors perished in Savannah's humid climate, but the cotton and peaches flourished. The garden was sold to

SIGHTSEEING IN SAVANNAH

Governor John Reynolds and was subdivided in the 1750s, becoming Savannah's first subdivision, but today it has been restored as Trustees' Garden Village, ringed by nineteenth-century brick and ironwork houses, with tiny jewel-like gardens. This, Savannah's first large restoration project, completed in 1950, heralded Savannah's renaissance. Here stands the Pirates' House, built between 1832 and 1850.

Savannah is renowned for its churches, magnificent edifices that reflect the soaring faith of the city's early settlers. Trinity Methodist Church, constructed of "Savannah grey" brick with a stucco finish, the oldest Methodist Church in Savannah, was dedicated in 1848 and is a valid example of Corinthian architecture, similar to that of Wesley Chapel in London.

Independent Presbyterian Church, an imposing Georgian Colonial structure, was designed by John Greene, of Rhode Island, in 1816 for a congregation organized in 1755. Fire destroyed the original building in 1889, but the present building is an exact duplicate of the original with its domed ceiling and elevated pulpit.

There is the columned First Baptist Church, whose congregation was organized in 1800. The present church was completed in 1833. And there is the Temple Mickve Israel, originated by a group of Spanish-Portuguese Jews who landed in Savannah five months after the founding of the colony, bringing with them a "Sephar Torah," which is ensconced in the present temple, built in 1878.

Wesley Monumental Methodist Church is a Gothic Revival memorial to John and Charles Wesley, founders of Methodism, who preached to the original settlers and whose memory is perpetuated in the breath-taking Wesley window, incorporating bust-length portraits of the two historic figures in its stained glass.

Savannah's loftiest sanctuary is the Roman Catholic Cathedral of St. John the Baptist, organized in 1799, a soaring French Gothic cathedral noted for its stained-glass windows executed by Innsbruck glassmakers in the Austrian Tyrol, its high altar of Italian marble, its unforgettable murals, its Sarouk Persian rugs, its chapel of the Sacred Heart, and the chapel and altar of the Blessed Virgin Mary.

The Lutheran Church of the Ascension, whose church is a Gothic sanctuary dominated by a magnificent Ascension window, was organized in 1741 by John Martin Bolzius of Ebenezer, who headed a colony of Salzburgers.

One of Savannah's most historic churches is Christ Episcopal Church, founded by the original settlers when Savannah was a Church of England settlement and served by such ministers as Henry Herbert, John Wesley and George Whitfield, who founded Bethesda Orphanage, which is still in operation today.

No visit to Savannah is complete without a view of Wormsloe Plantation, an eight-hundred-acre plantation estate on the Isle of Hope, which dates from the founding of Georgia in 1733, when it was granted to Noble Jones. Jones came to America with Oglethorpe in the original party aboard the ship *Ann*, accompanied by his wife and two children and two indentured servants. Jones was placed in command of Fort Wimberly at Wormsloe to protect Savannah against Indian and Spanish attack. The ruins of this fort, built of tabby, a mixture of solidified sand and oyster shells, remain today. So do some of the mulberry trees from the days when Wormsloe was used for the cultivation of silk. The gardens are an incredible sight, with thousands of towering azaleas and hundreds of camellias, native shrubs and live oaks.

The antebellum house is approached by a mile-long avenue of oaks and is flanked by the library that formerly housed the remarkable collection of Georgia history begun by George Wimberly Jones, who added the name De Renne, adapted from his mother's name, Van Deren. His collection includes such rarities as the original manuscript copy of the Constitution of the Confederate States; Jefferson Davis' private file of letters from General Lee, written during the War Between the States; and a number of Sherman's letters relating to the capture of Atlanta and Savannah, and is now in the University of Georgia Library. And there are also family portraits: Noble Wimberly Jones, by Charles Willson Peale; George Jones, by Rembrandt Peale; and portraits also of George Wimberly Jones and Wymberley Jones De Renne.

Visitors to the estate will want to see the family burial ground and the large Confederate battery.

Wormsloe is redolent of history. It has been successively handed down from father to son since Noble Jones, doctor, surveyor, planter, engineer and military leader, willed it to his son, "the morning star of liberty," Speaker of the House, Georgia legislator and member of the Continental Congress. From him it passed to Dr. George Jones, judge of the Superior Court and U.S. senator, and from him to Dr. George Wimberly Jones, who began the collection of Georgia history and willed it to his son, who established the Wormsloe Press, which printed many rare items in limited editions. Today the estate is owned by the Craig Barrow family, direct descendants of Noble Jones. While retaining the magnificent antebellum home and the library, they have turned over the major portion of the estate to the Nature Conservancy, which will in turn give it to the Georgia Heritage Trust, which will make it accessible to visitors.

A visit to Wormsloe is like a journey back in time, from the origins of the colony and the era of the Spanish menace to the days of plantation leisure, when men had the time and the means to accumulate great collections. The twentieth century has made no inroads here. More than any other site, Wormsloe is what Savannah is all about.

CHAPTER 16

Discovery

"THE BEST KEPT SECRET in America" is out now. Savannah has been discovered and she loves it. Like a beautiful woman once doomed by the vagaries of fate to obscurity, her face has finally emerged, and hundreds of journalists and artists and craftsmen are paying tribute to her charm, while industrialists from all over the country are courting her, impressed by the harbor tours aboard *The Waving Girl* at sunset.

Savannah woos her vistors with pageantry and festivals. Highlight of the year is, of course, Founder's Day, February 12, when the drama of the historic meeting between Oglethorpe and John Wesley, Mary Musgrove and Tomo-chi-chi is re-enacted on the waterfront. The week is marked by fairs, balls, candlelight dinners and a colorful parade in Colonial dress from Yamacraw Bluff to Oglethorpe's statue with a pause to lay a wreath at the monument to Tomo-chi-chi, who elected to be buried with the British after his sojourn in the English Royal Court. Savannah's St. Patrick's Day parade is the second-largest in the nation, with 42 bands and 184 units, a highhearted procession that has highlighted March 17 since 1820. Late March, the very peak of the city's spectacular spring, is marked by the annual Tour of Homes and Gardens, when the great hostesses of Savannah open their homes to the public and visitors can roam at will down brick walkways smoldering with azaleas and curtained by garlands of wisteria. Summer is initiated by the Blessing of the Shrimp Fleet, a sacred, colorful ritual performed by a Catholic priest at Thunderbolt, where the shrimp boats assemble decked with flowers and flags.

On the first-Saturday festivals, held monthly throughout the year, craftsmen and artisans from all over the Southeast bring their wares to the waterfront and display them on the ramps of their station wagons. It is a joyous spectacle. In the little pocket parks, combos are playing everything from Dixieland to rock-and-roll and crowds explore the Factors Walk Military Museum and the ships of the Sea Museum. They tarry in the ice cream parlor or at the outdoor Wine and Cheese Locker, run by one of many Northerners who came to the city as visitors and gave up burgeoning careers to make their way in Savannah. They cater to the natives and tourists who delight in shopping the waterfront's unique little shops and galleries for original paintings, custom-made furniture, gourmet cookware and imported coffee, teas and spices, handmade leather articles, brass, pewter and pottery made to order, handcrafted jewelry, Habersham Plantation furniture, original wicker and Rattan, shells, driftwood and nautical antiques, needlepoint, imported cigars and cigarettes, handmade toys, Scandinavian imports, primitive antiques and unique furniture individually handcrafted. And many venture on up to 221 East Bay Street to Bailey's Forge to see the extraordinary ironwork of Ivan Bailey, a Midwesterner trained in

Germany who is restoring much of the city's magnificent grillwork.

Daily, Historic Savannah and the Visitor's Bureau sponsor tours—walking tours, tours by bus, mini-train, bicycle and automobile equipped with tapes recording historic sites and events. And Bill Thompson, of Historic Savannah, is now arranging Saturday tours to Isle of Hope to view Wormsloe Plantation.

Not surprisingly, tourism has become Savannah's major industry. From 1963 to 1975, tourism in Savannah rose by 700 per cent, a direct result of the restoration effort. Says the National Park Service, which renovated Fort Pulaski in the late 1920s: Savannah possesses "exceptional value in commemorating or illustrating the history of the United States."

By 1975, according to Historic Savannah, restoration had resulted in a $40-million investment in the private renovation of historic properties, revitalization of the central business district, where some $1 million had been invested in new and renovated office space, and expenditures of more than $10 million in federal urban renewal funds for projects reinforcing the restoration movement. There had also been a rise of 239 per cent in families with incomes of ten thousand dollars or more from 1960 to 1970. And the unique, colorful, bustling new shops along the waterfront are directly attributable to the restoration movement.

Having proved effective in the early-historic district, the restoration movement has gathered new impetus with the efforts to save the Victorian district. Whole blocks of Victorian houses, most of them of the Carpenter design, have been renovated and are being rerented to the best of their tenants at a modest seventy-five dollars a month, in order to allay any major displacement of families, and a Victorian Square complete with gazebo had been created by Mills Lane.

The other facets of Savannah's new prosperity are industry, the Savannah port, and the military. A boon to Savannah's economic health during the next few years will be the buildup of the nearby Fort Stewart-Hunter Army Air Field complex. Some politicians are predicting this will sweep Savannah into the tide of one of the "greatest local economic surges" going on anywhere in the United States.

This is not blind optimism. The Hunter-Stewart payroll will climb from $48 million annually to more than $200 million by 1978 and the number of military and civilian employees and families will jump from eight thousand to at least forty thousand in 1977, meaning a major rise in the construction industry.

Also, some $52 million has been appropriated by the Georgia General Assembly for expansion of the port, which is now the major port between New Orleans and Baltimore.

"We think we have the potential of becoming a real distribution center," says Sanford Ulmer, director of the Savannah Port Authority. "With the physical facilities for handling ocean cargo in Savannah and with the advent of the completion of I-16 and I-95 and the two of them intersecting about ten miles from the heart of downtown Savannah, the trading area for the Georgia Ports Authority is a fan sweeping through the Midwest," he says.

Cargoes that formerly entered the United States through New York have started coming in through Savannah because of lower costs, says Ulmer.

Grumman American Aviation Corporation, one of the largest industrial employers in the area, is expanding its operation, bringing its Ohio plant to Savannah.

DISCOVERY

With the stunning new Civic Center attracting every type of cultural offering to the city, its fine symphony orchestra, the Telfair Academy of Arts and Sciences, and the oldest little-theater group in the United States, the arts are fairly exploding in Savannah. The city, though it is not without problems, is well into another golden era, a period that rivals her ascendancy in the cotton kingdom, but this time based on a sound relationship between the races, a diversified economy, and deep aesthetic roots. She has her flaws—what lady doesn't?—but she has learned to deal with them. "I love this city so much, I try to go to town by a different route every day so I can keep track of her changes," said Mayor John Rousakis in 1975, then in his second term of office.

Most of Savannah's lovers feel the same way. Lady Astor, who called Savannah "a beautiful lady with a dirty face," would have to eat her words today. Savannah still has deep scars from her long, abject depression, but they are healing, one by one, every day, and she is fast emerging as the prototype of American cities.